COMPL EMENT

**The Surprising Beauty of Choosing
Together Over Separate in Marriage**

In true Aaron and Jamie style, this book is real, raw, hilarious, and full of wisdom. They do not sugar coat the challenges of marriage yet invite married couples to discover the beauty and adventure God has purposed for our marriages. We need this book in this time and culture.

Nick and Christine Caine, founders of A21

Today's culture often alludes to marriage as a monotonous, contractual agreement that can easily be undone and reversed. Aaron and Jamie have delightfully intertwined their firsthand experiences to expound upon God's deepest desires for marriage. This book is for every couple who wants to do the hard work and intentionally live out their covenant.

Gabe and Rebekah Lyons, bestselling authors and cofounders of Q Ideas

As in all of life, the best marriage mentors are the ones who not only have a compelling message, but also a compelling life to share. Our friends Aaron and Jamie Ivey are such mentors who offer us their marriage "message" through the lens of Scripture. For who can tell us more about healthy, life-giving marriage than the Maker of marriage Himself? As Aaron and Jamie take us on this journey, they do so in a way that reveals their own life together. In the sharing of their lives as an illustration of their message, they provide a compelling path for other husbands and wives to follow. We cannot recommend *Complement* highly enough!

Scott and Patti Sauls, Christ Presbyterian Church, Nashville, Tennessee

The Colliers believe that in marriage, if you're not having fun, you're doing something wrong. Aaron and Jamie are having the most fun and teaching couples how to press through the messy middles of marriage to create a continual flow of synergy, together. In this incredible book, the Iveys are showing us how to be who we each were created to be while leaning on the power of Jesus to help us draw nearer to our spouses for a life of connection, clarity, and screaming-at-the-top-of-our-lungs cheering for the one you share forever with.

Sam and Toni Collier, lead pastors of Hillsong Atlanta

As this book says, "No one stumbles into marriage. It has to be built." We can so relate to this, and we wish we had this book in our hands a decade ago! What Aaron and Jamie do in *Complement* is point us to a biblical perspective of marriage that is centered on the faithful work of Jesus. They dig deep into their own marriage and into the Bible to give us winsome and vital truth that comes to life and can be lived out every day. This isn't a book to be read "some day"; you should read it today. As you do, you're going to be challenged, encouraged, and filled with hope.

Joel and Brittany Muddamalle, Proverbs 31 Ministries | Transformation Church

COMPL EMENT

The Surprising Beauty of Choosing
Together Over Separate in Marriage

Aaron Ivey

B&H
PUBLISHING
NASHVILLE, TENNESSEE

978-1-5359-9669-3

Published by B&H Publishing Group
Nashville, Tennessee

Published in association with Jenni Burke of Illuminate
Literary Agency: www.illuminateliterary.com.

Dewey Decimal Classification: 306.81
Subject Heading: MARRIAGE / HUSBANDS / WIVES

Unless otherwise noted, all Scripture is taken from The Holy
Bible, English Standard Version. ESV® Text Edition: 2016.
Copyright © 2001 by Crossway Bibles, a publishing ministry
of Good News Publishers.

Also used: The Christian Standard Bible (CSB), copyright
© 2017 by Holman Bible Publishers. Used by permission.
Christian Standard Bible®, and CSB® are federally registered
trademarks of Holman Bible Publishers, all rights reserved.

Cover design by B&H Publishing Group. Author photo by
Becca Matimba Photography @bmatimbaphoto. Texture by
HolyCrazyLazy/shutterstock.

It is the Publisher's goal to minimize disruption caused by tech-
nical errors or invalid websites. While all links are active at the
time of publication, because of the dynamic nature of the internet, some web addresses or links contained in this book may
have changed and may no longer be valid. B&H Publishing
Group bears no responsibility for the continuity or content of
the external site, nor for that of subsequent links. Contact the
external site for answers to questions regarding its content.

1 2 3 4 5 6 • 25 24 23 22 21

To our children: Cayden, Amos, Deacon, and Story Ivey

If God has marriage in His plan for your life
(and it's okay if He doesn't), we pray your
marriage is fun, thrilling, Jesus-honoring, and always
complementing each other throughout life.

Contents

Preface

We're so glad you picked up this book! We wholeheartedly believe that marriage is one of God's incredible gifts to us as His children. While it's not the ultimate thing in life, marriage is meant to be life-giving, thrilling, and beautiful for those who experience it.

We've been through sweet times and difficult times in the two decades of our marriage, and through it all we've learned that God designed marriage to be a living picture of His great love for His people. It's hard. It takes a lot of work, forgiveness, patience, and time. But we've found it to be worth it. And we want you to as well.

In a culture where marriage can be viewed as bland, archaic, or boring, we've found a better way. And it isn't because we do it all correctly or have some special brand of marriage that is unattainable for some. As we've studied God's Word and seen more of His faithfulness in our own lives, we've actually come to see that God's purpose in marriage is more surprising and exciting than we realized.

We believe in marriage. We believe in *your* marriage. We want it to be healthy and vibrant, fueled by the love of Jesus, and a powerful tool of mission in the world in which we live.

In this book, you're getting two perspectives on the same themes. We took the most valuable things we've learned about complementing each other in marriage, and wrote our unique perspectives on them. In fact, we didn't even read each other's portions of the book until in the late editing stages, so what you're getting is the raw, real, and vulnerable perspective on how we complement each other as we strive to honor Jesus with our marriage.

We'd encourage you to think of this not as two books, but two halves of the same book—and to read both halves. Read one half, then trade with your spouse. We think you'll find encouragement and challenges as you read both of our thoughts on each concept.

We're fighting for *your* marriage, even from a distance. It's an honor to join you on the journey of choosing together over separate in marriage.

Aaron and Jamie Ivey

What I Thought Marriage Would Be

Just wait 'til you get married. It's all downhill after that."
I can't tell you how many times I heard this spoken over me before marriage. Some said it to get a quick laugh, brushing it off as merely a joke. But sadly, I think others truly meant it.

It still saddens me when I hear people refer to the *best days* of their relationship with their spouse as the ones before they said, "I do." It's not the way it's supposed to be.

What was once a vibrant friendship and dating relationship, somehow becomes less thrilling, less spectacular. At least, that's what so many people assume.

Maybe you've heard someone half-jokingly say something similar. In the moment, it's easy to simply laugh it off and move on, but a bland marriage is far too common in today's culture. There's a painful truth about how many people view and experience marriage. To be fair, no one enters into marriage dreading it or hoping it will shift toward a lifeless, joyless, empty relationship. No one intends for their marriage to wear out and get stale. No couple hangs their wedding day photos on the wall of their first home and says, "Well, that was the best and last day of our fun relationship." Yet somehow it happens.

As a young single man, I always found myself scratching my head, wondering *why* that is the case for so many marriages. Before Jamie and I were married, I didn't see many marriages that were thriving and full of life. Sure, I saw some that were fully committed to each other, lasting thirty+ years, but none of them seemed to represent the kind of giddy, adventurous, passionate marriage that I had so hoped was possible.

Tom and Betty were an older married couple I remember seeing in church every week. Tom had a great job, one that required carrying a briefcase, wearing a suit, and boarding an airplane a few times every week. He drove a shiny Dodge pickup truck and parked it in a spotless garage in the suburbs of Houston. Every day at 5:30 p.m., Betty unearthed a crock pot full of red meat and potatoes as Tom walked in the door and sat down to a table set for two. Betty seemed unhappy and unfulfilled, but Tom seemed pretty grateful for the apron-adorned woman of his dreams. They stayed married as long as I knew them, but every time I saw them, they sure seemed unhappy. Somewhere along the way they had grown distant from each other, like two islands in the Pacific without a bridge or boat to ferry between.

I also remember looking at the marriage of my Uncle and Aunt. It seemed they had a pretty normal marriage. At least it seemed that way from my adolescent perspective. Their modest home was decorated with Bible verses and framed portraits of white-Jesus. He hung on the wall in the dining room, the hallway to the bathroom, and right above the TV in the living room. Try watching an episode of your favorite TV show with Jesus frowning down on you. It's weird. And just like the scowl on Jesus' face, they both had a frozen frown etched onto their faces as they lived their days and nights in the same house. Most nights, they ate dinner in silence like strangers, then wandered to their bedroom, crawled into two separate corners of their king-sized bed, and turned the lights off. They divorced after twenty-three years of marriage. The spark of love had dwindled, too dim to revive.

White-Jesus paintings couldn't save their passionless marriage.

I knew a pastor and his wife while in college who had what I believed to be a pretty typical marriage. He led, she followed. He ran the house, she cleaned the house. He led from a stage, she served in the shadows. She mothered the children, kept the laundry clean, and smiled at every church function. At the time, it seemed to be a totally normal Christian marriage. They were faithful to each other, they didn't fight, but they were rarely affectionate. There was an obvious shallowness to their friendship.

I remember eating dinner at their house one night. A wave of disappointment and sadness came over me as the meal ended and I got in my car to drive away. The conversation had only been about his ministry, what God was doing through him, and how he was leading his church. She sat silently at the far end of the table, uninterested, slowly spinning spaghetti noodles around her plate, then cleared the table as he continued to tell me more about himself. I remember that feeling so *off*. She had to have imagined more for their marriage on that sacred day where they recited vows, kissed, then ran down the wedding aisle to the church fellowship hall to celebrate with friends and family.

I stood as a groomsman at a good friend's wedding while I was in college. He was marrying the girl of his dreams. They were a super-fun couple, the kind that laughs at each other's jokes and finishes each other's sentences—no matter how annoying it is to everyone else. They were like magnets to each other. You never saw one without the other attached by the hand. As I stood with a close-up view of their wedding ceremony, I watched them place rings on one another's fingers, speak their vows, and stare goldenly into each other's eyes. I was so happy for them, but at the same time I couldn't help but feel a weird sadness, wondering if their love would dwindle and burn out as well. I mean, it was inevitable right? That's all I had seen in older marriages all around me. Was this what so many spoke of when they joked about marriage being the beginning of the end? As soon as the caterers and DJ packed up the wedding venue at the end of the night, would the fire I saw in my friends' eyes begin to slowly dissolve?

I certainly hoped not.

Not all marriages I saw were bad. I can remember several throughout the years that seemed to be beautiful.

A few couples seemed to be in love and giddy about each other. But, from my perspective, they were the rare oddballs, not the norm.

After a few failed dating relationships of my own in college, I finally met Jamie in the winter of 1998. I'll tell more of our story throughout the chapters of this book, but I'll say this now: she was altogether different than any woman I had ever met. She was dazzling. Jaw-dropping. As we became closer friends, I soon discovered that she had a loveliness about her that was far beyond her outward appearance (even though, let's be honest—she's gorgeous). Our friendship was intoxicating. I loved every second of being around her. Whether it was walking through the aisles of Target or eating chips and creamy jalapeño dip at Chuy's in Houston, Texas, we laughed as much as we talked. We talked about dumb things, we talked about serious things, and laughter was the thread between every conversation.

Younger guys often ask me, "How did you know that Jamie was the *one*?" I always answer the same way. And the answer is as earnest as it is simple. "I knew Jamie was the one when I couldn't imagine it *not* being her." I still feel that way about her. And now that we've been married for almost two decades, I can honestly say that our marriage is more fun, more life-giving, more fantastic than any year previous. We've had hard years, hard seasons, but I've never been able to imagine doing life with any girl but her.

When we began to talk seriously about marriage, we had so many conversations about what we wanted our marriage to be like. Of course, we talked about what kind of apartment we wanted, wondered where we would live, what our jobs would be in the future, and all the other mysterious things that come with embarking into an unknown future. But, more than those things, we found ourselves talking about *what kind of marriage* we wanted. The more we talked about it, the more we realized that we had the opportunity to build our marriage however we wanted.

Nobody stumbles into a thriving, beautiful marriage. You have to build it. Work at it. Nurture it. Dream it up and determine to do it right. When you start a marriage, you get to say, "Let's do it the better way! Let's not be content with a status quo marriage just because that's what most people we see have. Let's make it count, and let's have fun along the way!" So that's what we did.

I'll never forget one of the most powerful things Jamie has ever said to me. As we finished dinner at one of our favorite restaurants, she leaned in and casually said, "I'll go anywhere you go, as long as we go *together* and do it *together*." Wow. I'm not sure she even knew how profound that was in the moment. See, *there's a difference between going somewhere, and going together.* Most couples are going *somewhere*. But, one of the secret ingredients to a healthy marriage is going somewhere—*together.* Togetherness is as subtle and yet as powerful as salt in a pot of soup. Without the salt, you still have soup. But with salt, it's so much tastier—and much more fun to eat.

Togetherness is the salt of marriage.

You can try to do marriage without togetherness. You can try to wing it, hoping to stumble into a healthy and vibrant marriage. Some have been trying for decades. But when you discover the better way, you'll refuse to accept anything less.

I think I just want you to know that there's a better way than the status quo. God loves marriage. God loves singleness. God loves dating. God loves friendship. He's all in. And if He loves something this much, He wants you to love it also. It doesn't have to be "all downhill after that."

When I was a kid, I thought I might be a painter when I grew up. I took a lot of art classes in school, and the more I played around with watercolors and acrylic paints, the more I appreciated a great painting when I saw it on display. One of the most intriguing things about painting is that there's an endless supply of color options. Sure, there are primary colors that everything is built on—red, yellow, blue, black, and white. But from those simple five colors, you can create any color imaginable. There's no limit. No end in sight for what beautiful shades and tones you can create. And what's the magic that makes that possible? How can a few simple and primary colors unfold into literally billions of color palettes? The magic is in finding colors that complement each other.

Take a little red and little yellow and what do you get? The most gorgeous orange. Drag a little blue paint into a mound of yellow—you'll find a stunning green that can be used to paint leaves that blue or yellow alone could never conjure.

See, marriage is meant to be as thrilling and creative as painting with complementary colors. Sure, you are your own color, your own being. You are uniquely you, created perfectly by God and for God. And your spouse, or future spouse, is her own color, her own being, created by God and for God. But when God forges two lives together through the sanctity of marriage, those two colors complement each other in such a powerful and purposeful way that something crazy happens. A new color emerges.

Marriage is not simple arithmetic. It's not one plus one equals two. It's not Aaron plus Jamie equals Aaron and Jamie. No, it's something better than that! Marriage is one plus one equals *one*. A new one! A new identity is created—a color that didn't exist before. Aaron plus Jamie equals something much more powerful and vibrant than neither of us could be on our own. Just like painting, one color plus one color equals one brand-new, bold, stunning color. This is what a healthy marriage looks like. And just like a brilliant painting on display at an art museum, this kind of complementary marriage has the unique ability to

> Marriage is one plus one equals one.

display to the entire world just how good, and kind, and creative God is.

This is what happens when spouses choose to complement each other. Not change each other, not compete with each other, and definitely not fall into indifference with each other. Instead, brilliantly forming something much more beautiful than either person could be on their own. When that shows up on the canvas of your married life, people will be awestruck to see what's produced—something brand-new, something much better, something with purpose and insane beauty.

We decided early on to build our marriage on this: No matter what we do, who we become, what we run toward, what we work for, who we are ministering to, or where we are serving, we are going to do it *together. We are going to spend our lives complementing each other.* Bringing out the best in each other. Forging ahead with an earnest desire to bring out from the other person their best. To stand alongside, propping up, affirming, offering to the other what may be lacking, doing the hard work of complementing red with yellow, and yellow with red, until finally a beautiful hue of orange emerges—a color and tone much more vibrant than either person could be on their own.

When you lock arms with a spouse and decide to fight for that, your marriage will become salty and colorful in the way God intends. Not only will you find life and joy in marriage, but so will anyone who comes close. That's what God has in mind for every single marriage.

There have been a few times throughout the early years of marriage when I've wondered if we would end up like Tom and Betty, or my Uncle and Aunt. A few times it has seemed too good to be true, and I've found myself waiting for that little hiccup or bump in the road to spiral us into becoming merely committed roommates. But you've just got to believe I'm telling you the truth when I say this: Even in the hard seasons, we've been *together*. Even in the boring seasons of ministry, or what seemed like unfulfilling years of just treading water, we did it *together*. We were broke together. We were bored together. We've had thrills and failures together. We've won awards and embraced hurtful public criticism together. We've done it all together. Dedicated to complementing each other through it all.

This book isn't a treatise on how to have a perfect marriage—there's no such thing. And it's not a deep-dive into Aaron's and Jamie's perfect marriage, because that just ain't true. But we do want to plead with you to believe there's an alternative to a bland, lifeless, "it's-all-downhill-from-here" kind of marriage. It's the kind of marriage that Jesus really loves. It's the kind of marriage He wants you to have.

CHAPTER 1

Love

I don't remember the first time I told Jamie, "I love you."

I realize that makes me a pretty bad husband. Those are the things you're supposed to remember, right? Where you had your first date, the day and month of your wedding, where the first kiss happened, and that moment you asked the big question, "Will you marry me?" I remember *most* of those things, but I can't for the life of me remember saying for the first time the game-changing words that hurled the relationship into the *I love you* stage.

I'm sure when Jamie finally reads this chapter, she'll roll her eyes, recalling the exact moment, what she was wearing, the temperature of the room, and whether or not I seemed nervous or insanely confident. But I can't remember.

15

All that aside, I do know this with absolute certainty: I didn't know *how* to love.

I assumed loving someone was as natural as breathing oxygen, but it's not. We don't show up on the planet knowing how to love someone. Sure, we know how to like things such as food and comfort and safety. No one has to learn that. We know how to cry, how to laugh, how to complain, and certainly how to sin. And, even though we all have a *desire* to love, God designed humanity in such a way that *we'd have to learn how to love.*

During our engagement, Jamie broached a difficult subject with me. I could tell she had been brewing over something for a while. She seemed nervous as we sat in my Pontiac Sunfire in the driveway of her parents' house. I put the car in park, and although she reached for the door handle, she paused and sunk back into her chair. "I think we need to talk about something." Those are never the words you want to hear from someone you're dating, much less your future spouse, but I sunk into my chair and braced for whatever she had to tell me.

"I'm not getting from you what I need," she said without anger or judgment. "I feel like there are times where you just don't seem present. I don't *feel* like you're in love with me. I mean, I know that you say you are, but it doesn't always feel that way."

I knew exactly what she meant. I felt it, too. I mean, I was crazy about her. There was no doubt in my mind that I loved her and wanted only her to be the partner I ran with for the rest of my life. But I often felt like there was a giant wall between me and, well, not just her, but everyone. A wall too large to scale, and too thick to burst through. I undoubtedly wanted to love her, but I just didn't know how.

I knew enough about treating someone with kindness and respect. I was pretty good at that. I planned out dates with immaculate detail, making sure we had the most fun and the most epic experience each time. I got my car washed before each date night. I often showed up with flowers. I walked her to her front door at the end of the night, fought for purity in our relationship, said kind things from time to time, and had eyes for only her. But, that wasn't enough. And that's certainly not *love*.

It's possible to do all the right things, all the right actions, and not truly possess love. Love is certainly not less than action, but it's more. You can be faithful to someone without love. You can be nice to someone without love. You can even be engaged to someone and still need to learn how to love.

That was me.

I think love in recent decades has gotten much more confusing for us. In our over-sexualized age, it's become common to confuse attraction or infatuation with love. We assume love has to do with something we feel.

On the flipside, some Christians have rightly pushed back against that idea. Bible teachers and authors and marriage counselors have argued that love isn't merely a certain feeling, but a commitment—regardless of whether the feeling is there. But I think this falls short too; love isn't simply making a commitment to someone in a relationship.

The Author of Love has a lot to teach us about what love is, and what love isn't.

When Jamie finally got out of the car that night, I walked her to the door, hugged her with a tight grip, then drove home wondering how the heck I was going to figure out what love really was. I knew I didn't know how to do it on my own, but throughout the following weeks and months, as I began searching, the Holy Spirit started working a thought into my heart: I began to realize that it was going to be impossible for me to truly love Jamie until I believed I was truly loved by God. Truthfully, at the end of the day, I didn't believe God loved me.

Throughout my life, all of my biggest struggles shoot out from the same root. Whether it was years of being addicted to pornography, or years of feeling extreme loneliness and insecurity, it all came from the same place—not truly believing God could love me. And until that root issue was addressed, there was no way for me to love Jamie, much less anyone else.

I read a book while we were engaged that helped transform and correct my view of God and His love. A. W. Tozer's book *The Pursuit of God* helped shine a light beneath the surface of my heart, exposing the root that God so badly wanted to do surgery on. "What comes into our minds when we think about God is the most important thing about us," wrote Tozer. So many of my identity issues and love issues and sin issues stemmed from what I thought about God.

I assumed God was angry all the time, and when you think about God being angry, you can't help but live with a fear that he'll snap and suddenly crush you.

I assumed God was disappointed with me, and when you think this way about God, you'll spend every day of your life trying to out-work and out-impress every human you encounter.

If you think God is indifferent toward you, you'll be indifferent with yourself, and everyone else you're in a relationship with as well.

But when you begin to think rightly about God, everything changes. I think Tozer was right: what you think about God is the most important thing about you. And it's impossible to truly love anyone else if you don't first understand that God *is* love. He's not only the author of love, but He is love itself.

> It's impossible to truly love anyone else if you don't first understand that God is love.

First John 4:7–9 helped immensely as I was learning to understand God's love for me.

> Beloved, let us love one another, for love is from God, and whoever loves has been born of God and knows God. Anyone who does not love does not know God, because God is love. In this the love of

God was made manifest among us, that
God sent his only Son into the world, so
that we might live through him.

There is so much packed within those few verses. God is love. And love (true love) only comes from knowing and receiving the love of God. The Scripture is pretty clear that it's impossible to truly love someone without receiving and choosing to believe the insane love with which God has loved you. You can't muster up love. You can't conjure up love. You can't fake love. God's love has to be the root of your soul, the compass of your life, the rudder of your boat. Without it, you're just an action-based, performance-driven, feeling-fluctuating drifter. I was learning how true this was of myself. You can't truly love unless you are loved.

But there's also something specific about the love ascribed to God in 1 John. It says that He made His love known by sending His Son, Jesus, into the world.

There's never been anyone like Jesus, and there never ever will be. When Jesus burst onto the scene of the human story line two thousand years ago, it changed everything. There couldn't be another question as to *if* God loved people. That question had hung in the air for generations, as the people of God waited around for a Messiah to show up. Even if they believed in the laws of God and the truths of God, it was hard to know the love of God before they saw Jesus with their own eyes. As His feet strolled through dusty city streets and darkened alleys, His very existence proved that God's love was not merely a theory or religion, but it was active and on the move.

The Scripture says that "the love of God was made manifest among us" (1 John 4:9). Plainly put, the love of God showed up. It crashed through the walls of what everyone had ever thought about God. And when they got a glimpse of Jesus, they were peering into the very heart of God. And inside that big, beautiful heart is outrageous love.

One of the most distinguishing marks about the love of God is found in the *way* Jesus displayed His love. Sure, His love was spoken with His own words, it spilled out from everything He said, every parable and every peculiar story He told. But He chose an even better way to express His love, and this one is perhaps the most intriguing and countercultural thing about Jesus. It's the thing I'm most caught off guard by when I think of the King of the Universe coming to Earth and wrapping Himself in human skin.

Philippians 2 tells us that "though [Jesus] was in the form of God . . . [he] emptied himself, by taking the form of a servant. . . . And being found in human form, he humbled himself by becoming obedient to the point of death, even death on a cross" (vv. 6–8).

What? Jesus? The guy who was fully human and fully God, the Word made flesh, the Messiah, the Savior of the world, the King of kings, the Lord of lords? The form He deliberately chose as the greatest display of His love for us was being a *servant*? Countercultural. I told you. There could be nothing more humble than a servant. And nothing more humbling for Deity to do than take on the lowly role of serving people, all the way to death on a cross. And although I'm not fully sure why God would write the story this way, I do know this: There's no greater display of *love* than servanthood.

> There's no greater display of love than servanthood.

If we're ever going to learn what true love is, we have to get to the place where we are awestruck and deeply moved by the God who is Love. The One who came to serve us, not be served by us. When we think rightly about God, when we think this way when God comes to our mind, it will change us. Every relationship becomes about serving the other person because we've been served by God. Every dating relationship revolves not around *what can I get from that person*, but *how can I serve her*. Every marriage becomes not about getting our way, but about laying down our life, considering our life less important than the other person's, putting our own love on display through the form of humble servanthood. This is how Jesus did it. This is how He calls us to do it.

What about you? Do you know that you are loved? When you think about the cross of Jesus, does God's full and complete love grab ahold of you and shake you to the core?

This became a game-changer for me as I learned how to love. Slowly over time, God began to uproot the old disbelief that He didn't love me. He kindly replaced it with a better root. The more closely I looked at the person of Jesus, the more undeniable it became that I was fully and completely loved by God. And the more

I believed that, the more I could give my whole self to others, to Jamie.

I think that's what she was trying to say in the car so many years ago. She loved the fun date nights, the flowers, and the kindness and respect I showed her. But there was more she was after. She wanted *me*. She wanted to know me fully, to peer into my heart and soul as much as she could. And the only way I could ever give that to her was if I first understood the depth and width of God's love for me. On the cross, Jesus doesn't just say, "Here's all the things I've done for you," but rather, "I'm giving you all of me . . . I'm not holding back anything!"

One night in my apartment, I stumbled upon 1 John 4:11 and it shook me. And I've actually never gotten over it. It seems so simple at first glance, but like an iceberg in the ocean, the best parts are way below the surface, and it could take decades to fully explore and appreciate.

"Beloved, if God so loved us, we also ought to love one another." There it was. In plain view. The wall that stood between myself and Jamie, that wall that seemed too high and too deep, slowly began to crumble. It's like the more I leaned into God's love for me, the wall began to tremble and fall into rubble. If I were able to ever love Jamie in the way that she needed and deserved, I had to just make a choice to believe that God so loved Aaron. And if God so loved Aaron, I could finally be freed up to love without restraint, without fear, without hiding, without reservation.

Say it to yourself right now. "God so loved _____." Isn't that beautiful?

Whether you find yourself single, dating, or married, you'll never be able to love as fully as God intends until you rightly receive His love for you.

Do you realize how much God loves you? No one else compares to Him. No one can complete you or affirm you or like you quite like Jesus does. He has served you in the most radical way possible. He left heaven, wrapped Himself in human skin, stepped into an old busted town, then got His hands and feet dirty as He served every person He encountered. He served with His words, with His actions, but more importantly with His whole unbridled servant heart. Then, as if that wasn't enough, He served you by taking on every bit of your sin, shame, and sadness, and carried it to a cross, where He nailed it and Himself, then died. And then God raised Him from death making you clean and righteous before Him forever. Now, God sees you the way He sees Jesus. You are as secure as Jesus, as loved as Jesus, as cherished as Jesus. In doing all of this, Jesus forever sealed this incredible truth into your human story: He is love, and He loves you.

If He loves you this much, and if He lives in you, then you possess the uncanny ability to love someone in a way that the world has never seen. You have the ability to love someone relentlessly, forgivingly, through thick and thin, through miscarriage and infidelity, through disappointment and dysfunction, through sickness and tragedy. But only if you embrace the kind of love that comes from someone other than yourself.

"Jamie," I said on a date night a few months later. "I don't know how to love. Honestly, I don't think I've *ever* known how to love. But, I'm willing to learn. Because you're worth it. So, I'll put in the hard work, if you'll be patient with me along the way." That conversation was nearly two decades ago. And although I'm further along today than I was back then, I'm still learning how to love.

Maybe you too need to do some digging. Maybe you need to ask the God who is Love to give you a new root. A root that says, "I am deeply loved by God. And because of that, and only because of that, I can love in a way that looks like Jesus—a humble, dusty servant, relentlessly giving Himself away so others can find life and joy and love."

Imagine a marriage like that. There is no better way to complement your spouse than to come alongside her with the love that can only come from Christ Jesus.

> We love because he first loved us.
> (1 John 4:19)

CHAPTER 2

Serve

When did servanthood get such a bad rap?

I mean, does anyone really want to be known as a *servant*? There's nothing sexy or glamorous about serving. No one wins an award for "Servant of the Year," and we rarely applaud someone when we see them taking the lowly road of service rather than the upward road of power.

Maybe fear surrounds the word *serve* because it's been so mishandled in the past. Throughout the centuries of human existence, there have been some serious injustices that have distorted our understanding of this word. Servanthood has been abused, taken advantage of, and used to oppress people.

I think of the early followers of God in the Old Testament. They were enslaved to terrible rulers like

Pharaoh, where people were only a commodity owned by someone else in power. They were labeled "servants," and their lives were reduced to being bought and sold by the highest bidder. They didn't have any rights, no choices in life, and the heart of God grieved at His people being treated in this way.

But this story line didn't stop when Moses led God's people out of slavery and into the wilderness. For thousands of years since, the same story has been much the same. People owned people. The strong claimed the weak. In the culture in which the New Testament was written, it was far too common for humans to be indentured to other more powerful humans. Servants were the lowest class, the poorest, with terrible living conditions that often ended in death.

Even in our modern history, slavery has tainted nearly every single culture, tribe, and nation on the planet. It's like we cannot get away from the human condition that allows one person to see themselves as better and more powerful than another. From the atrocities of the early twentieth century in Germany, to the unimaginable terror of slavery in America, to genocide and trafficking and every other form of slavery still in existence today, there is this truth—the human heart has always wanted to classify people in two distinct categories: powerful and weak. Important and unimportant. Better and less. Worthy and unworthy. Master and servant.

And sadly, it has crept into our marriages as well.

I think this is why it's so hard for us view servanthood in the proper light. Why it's so hard to have a conversation about serving people, much less about serving a spouse. It sounds yucky. Serving someone triggers all sorts of very real baggage in our human story line, almost making it impossible to view servanthood as something to enjoy, aim for, and embrace with our whole

> The human heart has always wanted to classify people in two distinct categories: powerful and weak.

being. We hear "serve your spouse," and we assume it's a statement on power dynamics, or a declaration about dignity. One must contain more dignity or value, if they are to be served by the other, right? It's confusing, I know. And candidly, if one spouse is demanding servanthood from the other, we fall right back into the condition of our humanity we're all trying desperately to get free from.

Before you assume this chapter is going to be about how wives should serve their husbands, let me take the arrow from your hand. In marriage, my role is not to call Jamie toward serving me. She is called to be a servant of Jesus, first and foremost. My role is to relentlessly, passionately, joyfully, and perpetually serve Jamie. Whether she serves me or not, I want to have a heart that overflows with radical loving servanthood.

I want to be the most servant-hearted person my wife has ever seen.

I know this is a difficult conversation, because we've all seen it done so poorly in the past. You know the scenarios. The husband demands the wife serve him. He expects certain things to be done, and the scary word of "submission" soon finds its definition in petty things like homemaking, laundry, and a list of other things people have come up with. But that's not submission, and that's certainly not servanthood.

Maybe the scenario is flipped. The wife demands the husband serve her. She expects certain things to be done, and life to revolve around her. That's certainly not servanthood either.

We need a better example, a better scenario.

There have been countless people throughout the centuries who have stepped up and shown a better way to view servanthood. Dr. Martin Luther King Jr. spent most of his life preaching a gospel of love, service, and peace. There's a lot to learn from his example. Mother Teresa spent every waking moment giving her life away for the flourishing of other human beings, even those on their dying bed. We could all take notes from her heart of service.

There have been some beautiful examples of how God's view of servanthood actually transforms human hearts and brings life and joy like nothing else. Yet, in all the examples we could look at, no one has redefined and course-corrected servanthood more than Jesus Christ.

Jesus didn't simply address power dynamics or offer bits of advice on dealing with the mishandling of servanthood, He *became* the very thing that was so often misunderstood and taken advantage of—a servant. He became the example we all need by becoming an actual servant. His chosen posture as both Son of God and Son of Man was to lower Himself, forever proving that there is a massive difference between slavery and servanthood, and forever proving that there is not less power or dignity or worth in being a servant, but more.

Slavery has been and always will be wrong. Oppositely, servanthood has been and always will be the desired posture that God has for His people. And we'll never look more like Jesus than when we're serving other people.

I remember the first time I washed someone's feet. I was in college, and a fairly new follower of Jesus. (Side note—one of the most precious parts of being a new believer is you want to do every single thing that Jesus did. If He said pray more, you want to pray more. If He spent time with the homeless and the sick, you actually want to do the same. He went to the desert? Where's the nearest desert!)

When my college roommates and I stumbled across stories of Jesus washing people's feet, we naturally wanted to do the same. We planned a simple night of worship at the church I was attending, and after a few songs and times of prayer, we brought in several buckets of water and towels and took turns washing people's feet that had unknowingly walked into the strangest night of worship they'd ever been

> We'll never look more like Jesus than when we're serving other people.

to. Some were shocked and refused. Others bashfully took off their socks and cringed at the thought of someone seeing their un-manicured toenails.

It was awkward. Super awkward. Like, I can't articulate how awkward it was. For me and for the person whose feet I was suddenly six inches from. There's nothing comfortable about kneeling before someone as they remove their shoes and socks, holding their cold feet, washing their toes, then drying them with a towel. All while trying desperately to not make eye contact. Some of you reading this are dying at just the thought, because, let's be honest, feet are gross.

As strange as that moment was, I'll never forget the countercultural feeling I had as I mimicked Jesus doing what He so often did. Somehow, I didn't feel lowly at that moment. I didn't feel humiliated. I didn't feel less than the other person. I made the choice to serve awkwardly, and in doing it I felt empowered. I was strangely filled up with joy as I pushed past the bounds of what's socially acceptable toward what is Jesus-acceptable. Strange, I know.

I know that washing someone's feet is not the embodiment of serving people. My challenge is not for you to go give someone a foot bath. We need to serve people not merely with towels, but with actions, deeds, and words.

But at the same time, "washing someone's feet" was the action Jesus chose as a living symbol of a willing, joyful posture of service. Jesus wants us to see visually what our heart's posture should always be. It's like He took a quick photograph of what kind of heart He wants us to have, and said "Do this!" So, don't miss it. Stare at the photograph. Look closely at it. Servanthood is meant to look like this in and through your life. You are meant to joyfully and intentionally choose a humble posture— sometimes an uncomfortable posture—so that anyone you serve can ultimately see a snapshot of the heart of Jesus.

And if there is one person on the planet who should see this posture displayed over and over through you, it's your spouse.

No one should out-serve you when it comes to your spouse. No one should be more attentive to the ways she needs to be served, nourished, and cared for. No one. Period.

But, it requires a few things from you.

First, serving your spouse well requires a shift in thinking about what servanthood is and what servanthood isn't.

When Jamie and I were first married, I assumed the all-too-common way of servanthood. I thought serving her was simply doing whatever she didn't want to do. If she didn't like taking out the trash, I'd serve her by doing it. If she didn't like making the bed, I'd make it. If she didn't like to put gas in the car, I'd drive her car to the gas station and fill it up. Those things are all forms of servanthood, but I quickly found out that I could crush that to-do list without actually having a sincere heart of willingly, joyfully, and intentionally loving her.

I quickly slumped into doing tasks for her with a numb heart. At the end of the day, she didn't need a "servant" around the house simply doing tasks, she deserved so much more. Serving without a posture of love is simply task-management. And no one wants a spouse who simply checks tasks off from a list.

Second, serving your spouse well requires knowing your spouse.

There are things that are meaningful to Jamie, and there are things that are not. It took many years for me to discover how she receives love. She's not a gift girl, and I wish I would have known that early on. It would have saved a lot of money! She likes flowers, but flowers don't make her feel served and treasured. She likes it when I pick up the living room and put the throw pillows back on the couch, but that doesn't make her feel served and valued. The more I got to know her, the more I realized what truly makes her feel like I'm washing her feet.

She's a quality time girl. Completing all the house chores in the world doesn't even come close to a three-hour date night, where it's just me and her talking about real-life stuff. There's something about leaving the kids at home, pulling out of our driveway, and muting the notifications on my phone that communicates to Jamie, "I want to simply be with you." This is one of the primary ways that Jamie feels loved, and that she sees me serving her. It's uncomfortable for me to turn off my phone. It feels weird to me to stop working at night and simply be with her. But, that's part of what servanthood looks like. And it took me knowing that about her, and adjusting everything, to communicate that she is a treasure.

Third, serving your spouse well requires considering your spouse more important than yourself.

Who's most important in a marriage? The husband or the wife? Well, it should depend on who you ask.

If you ask me, I'll tell you that Jamie is the most important person in the relationship. And, I'm sure that if you ask her, she'll tell you that Aaron is the most important person in the relationship. I know the math doesn't add up, but this is the way servanthood works. Power dynamics dissolve when both people are making a conscious decision to say, "I consider you more important than myself." It's not, "I'm going to serve you as long as you are serving me." It's, "I'm going to serve you because you're more important than me!"

And when two people are saying this to each other, it becomes something rare and beautiful.

This is the resounding theme of Paul's words in Philippians 2:3–4 when he writes about the power dynamics of Christ and His people. He says, "Do nothing from selfish ambition or conceit, but in humility count others more significant than yourselves. Let each of you look not only to his own interests, but also to the interests of others."

What is the opposite of selfish ambition? Counting the other person more significant. That means, when given the choice, I choose Jamie's interests over mine. When given an option, I choose what makes Jamie feel loved and treasured over what makes me feel loved and treasured. And when both people in a marriage are doing this, there is power. There is freedom. The true and better picture of servanthood emerges.

That's why Paul would finish this statement by saying: (my paraphrase): "Have *this* mind among yourselves . . . because *Jesus* did this . . . He emptied Himself, by taking on the form of a *servant*." If anyone in human history has ever had the right to say, "Serve me," it was Jesus. But the only one who has a right to say that, instead said, "I've come not to be served, but to serve and lay down my life for you."

There is no way to have true joy in marriage without servanthood. It can't be done. Not only will you find absolute freedom by serving your spouse willingly and intentionally, you'll also find the greatest amount of joy. True joy comes from serving other people.

It's not easy, and it's certainly countercultural. The way up is the way down. The way forward is the backward way of taking a towel and washing the feet of your spouse. Over and over. Day by day. When both people embody this form of Jesus-like servanthood, no one will be oppressed or come up empty. It will always lead to freedom and life.

CHAPTER 3

Cheer

I remember the way it made me feel to hear her speak the nicest things in the world to me.

She went on and on about how talented I was, how nice I was, and how meaningful I had been in her life as a songwriter and pastor. The words felt good. Real good. They were incredibly gracious and over-the-top nice. But there was a problem.

She wasn't my wife. She was someone else's wife.

We stood side-stage after a worship service for only a few minutes, but as she placed her hand on my elbow and continued encouraging me, it suddenly struck me how dangerous it can be to receive more verbal affirmation from anyone who's not your spouse than from your spouse.

I assume this woman was just being kind, and I was grateful she took the opportunity to speak a word of encouragement. When someone has a meaningful impact on your life, you should tell them!

But after that exchange, I realized how powerful it is to be cheered on by someone. I'm a "words of affirmation" guy, so naturally, words mean the world to me. If we're all honest with ourselves, words mean the world to every single one of us. It may not be the highest value, but it's certainly something that counts.

I told Jamie about the experience, and I think it was one of the most important conversations we've ever had. I didn't like how much I liked that verbal affirmation. And, at the end of the day, I really wanted to hear it from Jamie. More than anyone else, I want my spouse to encourage and cheer me onward.

Jamie isn't a musician. She doesn't know the difference between a melody and harmony. She doesn't know what a note is, much less a key, or chord progression. She doesn't know many of the song titles of songs I've written. And I swear, if you asked her the difference between a good song and a bad song, she wouldn't know.

I'm not a sports fan. I don't know the difference between a running back and a lineman. I don't know who most famous athletes are. And I swear if you asked me what a sports analyst does, I'd ramble for about ten minutes trying to make something up, then have to Google "sports analyst" before having any sort of good answer.

We are not into all of the same things. I think of melodies every day, and schedule out live music shows I want to see. She thinks of interviews every day, and can hang with the boys during every single football game, knowing all the plays, all the calls, and the names of most of the best players. She has season tickets to University of Texas games, and I have tickets to every Austin City Limits Festival. She releases a podcast every week, and I release albums every year.

Jamie and I don't speak the same language, and we're not into the same things. But we've decided to do our absolute best to cheer each other on, even when we don't understand the intricate details of the other person's passionate interests. And you know what? It takes work, intentionality, and words.

As Jamie and I have processed our desire to be each other's biggest cheerleader, we often remind each other that no one should out-cheer our spouse. If I were to never hear kind, affirming, encouraging words from my spouse, it would make moments like that one with the "fan" incredibly dangerous. My heart would swell. I would crave it more and more. Words do that. If Jamie were to never hear positive and beautiful words of admiration from me about her job and what she does, it would be easy for her to find encouragement from social media and fans after a live event. But when both spouses agree to be each other's biggest cheerleader, nobody else's words can compare.

As we aim to complement each other, Jamie and I have made a serious determination to cheer each other on in life, both publicly and privately. And it's made a massive difference in how we interact with each other, and what is able to puff up our heart, and swell our pride.

> When both spouses agree to be each other's biggest cheerleader, nobody else's words can compare.

I guess I want you to hear this—*words matter*. You can't truly have a marriage that complements each other if you don't compliment each other. (There it is, the chapter was begging for it!) And, I'm not talking about cheap compliments either.

I'm talking about owning the fact that your words are powerful. Words have the power to degrade and squash people, but they also have the power to lift people up and send them soaring. You can't take words for granted. And whether you want to admit it or not, someone will encourage your spouse. It will be someone at work, or someone at the gym, or someone online. But, it will happen.

Most affairs don't start by casually making out with a stranger. They don't usually start with just a desire for sex, but a desire to be known, understood, admired. Most affairs (either emotional or physical affairs) start by someone taking the place of the spouse by speaking words that the other person is desperate to hear.

The human heart can't help but crave verbal affirmation. And when there is a void of verbal affirmation in marriage, a wide-open door exists, making it all too easy for anyone to walk right in and speak a word of encouragement that blossoms into much more than anyone ever expected.

So, why not make an intentional effort to never be outdone in speaking highly of your spouse? Why not do whatever it takes to find opportunities to give the life-giving words of encouragement to the one you've made a covenant with to endure with until the end? Perhaps we fail to do this because we don't understand the power of encouragement.

By definition, the word *encouragement* means to "place courage," to put into someone else the valuable and life-changing element of courage. In his book *The Furious Longing of God*, Brennan Manning writes: "Lodged in your heart is the power to walk into somebody's life and give him or her . . . *the courage to be*. Can you fathom that? You have the power to give someone the courage to be, simply by the touch of your affirmation."[1]

We cannot downplay this power! You have the power to walk into your spouse's life and give him or her courage. Can you believe that?

Simply the "touch of affirmation" as Brennan Manning describes it, changes your spouse. It changes her view of herself, her belief in her gifting and calling, and her firm belief that you are *for* her. And if it's not you, it will be someone else. Everyone possesses this power. So, if you're not the one choosing to empower your spouse, you need to know that someone else will

---

[1] Brennan Manning, *The Furious Longing of God* (Colorado Springs, CO: David C. Cook, 2009), 93–94.

come along and place courage in them. It only takes a short, side-stage conversation.

I don't mean to scare you, but instead, I want to free you up to be your spouse's biggest cheerleader.

I find the creation story so interesting, as God fashioned both man and woman. Do you know what the very first words ever recorded by man were? You remember the story. God made the world, then made man, then made woman. And as soon as Adam saw Eve, his mind was blown, and he spoke the very first words ever recorded in human history.

Imagine the beating of Adam's heart and the dropping of his jaw as he said,

> "This at last is bone of my bones
>   and flesh of my flesh;
> she shall be called Woman,
>   because she was taken out of Man."
> (Gen. 2:23)

The very first words of man recorded is what he said about his wife. And they are poetic words of praise, delight, euphoria.

Adam was the first cheerleader. Wow!

We've all sat at awkward dinners with other couples. You know the ones I'm talking about? Where one spouse speaks down about the other? It's subtle in the moment, but it directly contradicts the confidence and security that should be baseline in a marriage. When a spouse speaks down to another in public, it erodes the safety of being fully known and fully loved. If Jamie were to speak sarcastically or flippantly about me while in a public setting, it would slowly feel like she's weaponizing my weaknesses for a quick laugh. Too often, we don't realize how these subtle interactions can deflate vulnerability and weaken the bond of togetherness we should try to affirm, rather than destroy.

Public affirmation is as important as private affirmation. Jamie and I make an effort to never degrade or speak poorly about the other in public. Never. You'll never have dinner with us and hear one of us throw the other person under the bus. It's not being fake, and it's not hiding what we're really thinking. We've just decided this—I'm going to choose to uplift you with words, not push you down. I'm going to place courage in you, rather than steal courage by making you feel humiliated or embarrassed. And in two decades of marriage, I'm telling you—it works.

I'm not perfect. And I don't deserve to have a wife who sees the best in me. But, as she highlights the best parts of me in private and in public, it only makes me want to be a better person. It doesn't produce pride. It makes me think, *Wow, if this woman thinks highly of me, I only want to aim higher.*

Does your spouse deserve this from you? Maybe not. They may be in a tough season or walking in disobedience far from God. They may be living in sin or chasing other things than God. But, because Christ has loved and served you, you now possess the power to find something in them, and place in them the courage to be more than who they are today.

A few years ago, Jamie and I walked through a difficult situation with a married couple, friends of ours. After years of hiding a secret addiction to pornography, the husband finally brought it to the light and confessed to his community and his wife. We all know that pornography causes devastation, and as Jamie and I walked through this situation, we saw the effects of that devastation in both the husband and the wife. Trust had clearly been betrayed. The wife obviously felt lied to, confused, and wondered why she hadn't been enough. It was an impossibly hard situation.

As the husband's heart began to soften through confession, repentance, and accountability, her heart became bitter. She began to speak poorly of her husband to friends and community members. From a place of real hurt, she began to weaponize her husband's failures. It wasn't until she realized she, too, had to show her husband grace and forgiveness that she was able to reconcile and experience healing in the marriage.

Perhaps these are some of the hardest times to be a cheerleader for our spouse. It doesn't feel natural to speak highly of someone who has failed or messed up, does it? But, we believe that in these moments, these harder moments, forgiveness and grace can actually deepen the bond of marriage. It doesn't mean you write it off, or just flippantly skip by it, however it does mean you choose not to publicly speak of your spouse as an enemy.

There have been many moments that Jamie has disappointed me, not met my expectations, or hurt me in very real ways. But even in those moments, I must choose to never speak of her poorly. I can't throw her under the bus, no matter how tempting it may be. I have to look for the good, admire her repentance, and keep cheering her on toward Jesus, especially in public.

What if you owned up to this power, and instead of thinking less of your spouse, chose to find ways to think more of them? What if you decided to place in them the courage to be godly? Or the courage to be more honest? Or the courage to be more humble? It starts with just a few words. "I see this in you. And I want you to know it's amazing. Keep going." It's as simple, profound, and life-altering as that. It's lodged in your heart, so let it loose and use your words.

Your words have the power not only to bless, but to place courage in your spouse. So, without reservation, find every opportunity to cheer him or her onward. If you don't, someone else will. And you can't have a complementary marriage without complimenting the heck out of your spouse.

CHAPTER 4

Lead

eader is a strange word, isn't it? It can instantly conjure all kinds of thoughts and connotations—from inspiration and courage to fear and disgust—all depending on the kinds of leaders you've been around.

Whether it's a boss, a minister, a principal, or a parent—many of us have been wounded by leaders. I can vividly recall things spoken over me by bad leaders throughout my life. Not all were ill-intentioned, but it's crazy how a leader can say or do something that has lasting effects on our confidence, psyche, and our view of self.

"Aaron, you're just not the kind of guy that people will want to follow," a leader said to me in my college years. That stung. Sure, I'm a different person today than I was when I was twenty-one, but I'd be lying if I told you that phrase doesn't still flare up in my head, especially during tough times of leadership.

On the other hand, I can remember words that good leaders have spoken over me that to this day keep me moving forward, firmly believing the calling that God has on my life.

The word *leader* is a tough word. And when we think of leadership in the context of marriage, all kinds of flags get thrown into the air. Some of you may have cringed when you saw the title of this chapter, wondering how in the world we would tackle leadership in the context of marriage. I'd love for you to press in here and not write me off, because I hope that you'll see how beautiful God's plan for leadership in marriage truly is.

The best leaders I know are the ones who are constantly submitting to a higher leadership. Leadership becomes abusive when it's unrestrained, unbridled, and isn't submitted to any kind of higher authority. That's why we've seen so many people severely wounded by leaders in the church, in marriage, and in the workplace. Leaders who aren't accountable to authority are dangerous, and they can be incredibly hurtful to those they're called to care for. But, when you pair confident leadership with radical submission, not only is the leader healthy, but everyone around him or her thrives and finds joy and contentment.

I'll be honest. I've never *felt* ready for leadership—any kind of leadership, really. I've never felt strong enough to lead a church, much less lead my own bank account or manage a household with tiny human beings living in it. I wasn't ready for parenting. I wasn't ready for marriage. I still don't feel adequate to lead a team of artists and world-changers in Austin, Texas. And most days I don't even feel capable of leading my own emotions and life-choices.

> The best leaders I know are the ones who are constantly submitting to a higher leadership.

But maybe that's the kind of leadership God is pleased by—the kind of leadership that doesn't rely on *feeling ready for it.* What if that's the kind of posture that God enjoys most in a leader?

I've found that when you're utterly dependent on a Better Leader than yourself, you realize just how incapable you actually are of accomplishing, directing, inspiring, building, or leading anything at all. And, I think that's the way God wants it.

There are countless "bad leader" narratives in the Scriptures. In the Old Testament we read of many bad kings, ones who led from arrogance and pride, greed and gain. Those leaders didn't empower or edify the ones they led, but instead brought oppression and sorrow upon their people.

> When you're utterly dependent on a Better Leader than yourself, you realize just how incapable you actually are of accomplishing, directing, inspiring, building, or leading anything at all.

Leadership requires a massive underfunding of pride. If pride is currency in the bank of the human heart, leadership requires not only cutting back on pride, but deleting it from the budget completely. Prideful leaders are the worst kind, but humble and submissive leaders look a lot like the person of Jesus.

When Jesus stepped into human history, we see the stark contrast of humble leadership. His way was much different. He was the essence of humble confidence. Strong, yet completely dependent on His father. Wise, yet meek. Bold, while also kind. He was a phenomenal leader, one to be revered at every bend, yet He consistently pointed again and again to His heavenly Father. Even Jesus, the greatest leader that has or ever will exist, was completely submissive to His Father, even all the way to death on a cross.

To whatever degree you feel like you've surrendered or achieved submission, I guarantee you haven't taken that all the way to death on a cross. So, there's something to learn here! Something to be inspired by. Something to look at and mimic.

There is no such thing as good leadership without great submission.

Sometimes, when we think of marriage we tend to oversimplify leading and following—one person is the leader of the marriage and the other person is the follower of that leader. But I don't see any kind of leadership that can be void of followership. Likewise, I see that every person is called to some sort of leadership in their lives. It's too simplistic to look at marriage and say one person is a leader, and the other is simply a follower.

Let me explain.

"There can only be one leader in the marriage," said one of our leaders while Jamie and I were walking through engagement. "And, Aaron you're the *only* leader in the marriage. Are you ready for that kind of leadership?" I remember getting hot and sweaty, super nervous by not only the question, but by the enormous weight that came with my timid answer in his wood-paneled office.

"Yes?" I said, slightly lifting my voice to give an unintentional question mark at the end of the word.

I secretly wondered how in the world I would ever be able to carry the ultimate weight of leading a wife, potential future children, a household, a Bank of America account, maybe a mortgage in the future, a couple of cars? A minivan? I've heard maintenance on those is endless. Shoot, we'd probably get a few dogs at some point, too. That seemed like a lot of work. And time. Jamie loves dogs. I'd be the leader of them, too? And what about bills? So many bills, right? And financial planning? Retirement, 401K, home repairs, making sure there's food in the fridge, big life decisions, taking care of parents when they get old, replacing a roof on a future home?

Oh my goodness. There can only be *one* leader? And it's on *me*? What's Jamie's role in this?

"And Jamie, your role is to submit to Aaron, your leader," he said, turning to her. "Are you ready to take on that sort of posture?"

I'm not sure what Jamie's response was in that moment—I'm sure it was godly and good. And, I also know this leader wasn't being cruel or even speaking something contrary to Scripture. It's pretty clear in the Bible that while husbands and wives are created with equal amounts of dignity, worth, and value, there is some clarity on differences in roles (Eph. 5:22–24).

But I wonder if, like that leader during our engagement process, we've oversimplified what it means to lead and what it means to submit. I wonder if we've somehow made leadership all about making the decisions, and submission all about going along with the flow. I wonder if we've even over-simplified the whole thing by saying only the husband leads, and only the wife submits. Surely, there's more to it? Surely there's something more beautiful about what God has in mind when He forges two human beings in covenant marriage.

In fact, when you look at the Scriptures, there's a clear calling for *both* husband and wife to lead in different ways, and an absolute calling for *both* husband and wife to fully submit. Maybe that's where we've allowed confusion to muddy the waters a bit.

Oftentimes, when quoting the famous "submission" passage of Scripture in Ephesians 5, we skip over perhaps the most important part. The Bible points out first that we must be "submitting to one another out of reverence for Christ" (v. 21). That goes for all Christians. Above all, then, both husband and wife are called to submit to each other, as fellow believers, out of reverence for Jesus. You can't have healthy submission in marriage if each person is not first submitting wholly and completely to Jesus. Both spouses are implored to submit their whole lives to Jesus Christ as the Leader of the marriage. It's the only way it can work.

I'll say it this way. Although Jamie and I do have particular roles in marriage and life, we're both called to lead and follow in many different ways and relationships. We both lead our children, teams of people in our jobs, and we use our unique talents and gifting to lead by serving others. But we're also called to submit to our church leadership, elders, and ultimately and primarily to Jesus.

Jamie is one of the best leaders I know. She leads an amazing staff at Ivey Media (her podcast, book writing, and event company). She leads our children better than

I do on most days. She speaks to hundreds of thousands of people on a weekly basis through The Happy Hour Podcast with Jamie Ivey. She leads people to follow after Jesus, to follow their God-inspired dreams, to give their life away for the gospel. Further than that, she has led our marriage in countless directions that I would have never considered—adopting three children, moving to the country, and giving our resources generously to those in need.

I hope Jamie could also say that I'm one of the most submissive people she's ever met. I submit to my fellow elders. I submit to the Spirit's moving and stirring. I submit to authority that is above me in my church, and I hope it can be said of me that I submit, to the best of my ability, to my Savior, Jesus Christ—what He wants, where He tells me to go, and what He wants of me.

Jamie is a leader. Jamie is submissive.

Aaron is a leader. Aaron is submissive.

Full disclosure, that leader in our engagement got it absolutely right—*there can only be one leader in the marriage.* There can't be two leaders with any healthy functioning team. Anyone working or serving with two coleaders knows the complexities and unhealth that can arise when no one knows where the buck stops, if you will. There can only be one leader.

But in our marriage that *one leader* is not me. I'm not the leader of the marriage. That's too much pressure. Too much hinging on me.

There can only be one sole leader, and His name is Jesus. He's the King of our marriage. He's the Lord of our relationship. He's the Ruler of our household. He's the only one that gets the elevated title of Leader of Aaron and Jamie's marriage.

This concept has the ability to radically change the health and purpose of marriage—specifically, your marriage or future marriage.

As you read this, you're probably thinking, *C'mon, Aaron. That sounds a little churchy. It sounds like a massive cop-out. Like, for real though, who is the leader of your marriage—you or Jamie?* I know it sounds idealistic and maybe a tad religious. But it's neither.

> There can only be one sole leader, and His name is Jesus.

"So, what is your role, Aaron? You're not

the leader. Okay, I get it. Then, what is the role of the husband?"

I don't want to dodge the question. I have no intention to leave you hanging, nor do I want to make you think Jamie and I just wade through marriage without clarity of our roles (even though that's sometimes not as clear as everyone would like). And while I do have the role as husband to take the lead in the spiritual health of our marriage and home, caring for our family, helping us resolve hard family decisions, I am not the ultimate leader.

If you peel back the layers of any healthy, vibrant, biblical marriage, you can't get away from this reality—if Jesus is the Lord of a marriage, it just works. It works as it's intended. Things fall into place. Roles make sense. Leadership and submission collide into something beautiful.

It'll still be hard—lots to work out—but when you have a leader like Jesus, and both husband and wife are submitting to His authority, at the very least you have something that looks more like what Paul was referring to in the book of Ephesians. Further, Jamie and I have found it to be one of the secret ingredients to a fun, fulfilling, adventurous, and healthy marriage and home.

So, here's what I think the role of a godly husband should be. Or another way of saying it—here's what I see the Bible telling husbands to be in a healthy, beautiful, Jesus-honoring marriage.

Husbands, you *are* called to be the leader, but not in the controlling, authoritative, unbridled, unsubmitted way we've seen from too many leaders. There's a better way. A more beautiful way. A life-giving way.

Husbands, you are called to be the Lead Submitter. You take the first step toward submission to God, not her. You lead out on what submission looks like. You model and exemplify to your home, whoever may live there, what it looks like to be fully submitted to the authority of Jesus Christ, your ultimate leader.

Ephesians 5:25 says, "Husbands, love your wives, as Christ loved the church." How did Christ love the church? By submitting to the will of His Father to die on the cross. By submitting His very life for the forgiveness of our sins.

This may come as a surprise to you, but Paul never actually said to *lead* your wife; he said to *love* her. That starts with looking to Jesus, and submitting to Him in your life and your marriage.

Husbands, you are called to be the Lead Servant. You make the first move toward being servant-hearted, not her. No one in your household should out-serve you. You should be the first to lay down your life, to serve when it's uncomfortable and inconvenient. You have the wonderful opportunity and calling to model to your wife what the serving hands of Jesus actually look and feel like. Ephesians 5 also says that Christ gave Himself up for the church. Just as Jesus served *first,* husbands should make the first move of service.

Husbands, you are called to be the Lead Lover. Have the courage to love when it's hard. And you do it first. Pursue when it's not reciprocated or earned.

No other person should show more affection, give more verbal affirmation, or show more love through action than you. What a privilege to able to model the love of Jesus to your spouse, anyone in your home, and every person you come in contact with.

One more thing to point out from Ephesians 5 is that husbands are called to *love* their wife as they love their own bodies. Paul speaks of nourishing and cherishing your wife, just as Jesus leads in nourishing and cherishing His bride, the church.

Listen, that kind of leadership goes beyond social norms, stereotypes, and abused versions of leadership we've all seen. And when your spouse sees this kind of leadership—one that is fully submitted to God, and is not manipulating or demanding—it's otherworldly. The way God intended it to be.

CHAPTER 5

Follow

I can't tell you how many times I have followed Jamie's lead.

God has a unique way of speaking to Jamie, telling her to do crazy things, like adopt children from Haiti or start a podcast to empower women (when podcasts weren't really a thing . . . not even your iPhone had a podcast app back then).

"I think we should adopt this precious boy from Haiti," she said as she slumped into the couch in our tiny home in Murfreesboro, Tennessee. I had just put Cayden and Deacon to bed, after an hour or so of wrestling them toward sleepiness.

"Um . . . okay . . . he is in fact precious," I said as I saw a photograph of his malnourished and sick body in a bed of a rescue center just outside of Port-Au-Prince, Haiti. "But, we just adopted Deacon, right?"

"Yes, but I don't think God's done with our family," she said without hesitation.

I looked around our tiny two-bedroom home, noticed the small wooden dinner table with four chairs, and thought of the immense financial responsibility that would come with not only the adoption process, but also with adding another human being to the Ivey household.

"I just don't think we have the room," I said bluntly. "Or the money. And, Jamie, honestly . . . where would he sit? We only have a dining room table that seats four!"

As soon as the words came out of my mouth, I realized how silly they were. I knew she was right about us adopting Amos. There was a glaring need in front of us. And that need had a photograph, a name, and was now filling up the entire screen of Jamie's laptop as she waited for my response. That little boy had no family. He didn't care about dining room tables, where he would sit, tiny suburban homes, or how much money it would take to get him into our home.

Jamie was right. So, I followed her lead.

Following isn't always easy. Sometimes following seems incredibly countercultural, especially in our male dominant culture where most of us grew up hearing, "Don't be a follower, be a leader!" Following is frowned upon. It's seen as weakness. We encourage people to be strong, powerful, wise—not *following* the leader, but *being* the leader.

But the way of Jesus has always been marked by an undeniable request to follow. "Will you follow me?" He asks. "It will change everything about you, and potentially everything about the world. But you have to choose. Will you follow me?"

I wonder if people thought it was crazy back in the day that Jesus would flip leadership so drastically, making a willingness to follow the first requirement for leadership. I read through the Gospels a few months ago, and I counted how many times Jesus said, "Follow me." It was mind-blowing how even when Jesus was calling ordinary people to great leadership, He started by calling them to extraordinary follower-ship.

> You can't ever lead anything without first following.

Leading and following were inseparable in His mind. You can't ever lead anything without first following. Following isn't a dig on your dignity or strength. Dignity and strength are actually amplified when we humbly follow.

I'm called to follow Jesus, obviously. At one point, just like He did to every disciple, He said to me: "Aaron, I want you to come follow me. But it's up to you." I said yes, and I'm so glad I did.

But there are also times when I follow the lead of my peers because they know something I don't know. They have a perspective I don't have. Countless times I've followed the lead of people that I'm technically responsible to lead or supervise. They usually have better ideas, new ways of doing something I haven't considered, or a unique perspective I haven't considered. So, I cheerfully follow their lead. And it makes me no less of a leader. It actually makes me a better leader.

The same is true in marriage. Following the lead of my wife in many scenarios throughout the years, I've learned, too, that following her never downplays my role as husband. It actually strengthens it. And it strengthens our marriage.

CHAPTER 6

Fight

I hate being wrong, and I love being right.

I don't know how it all started in me, but I've always had an aversion to admitting I'm wrong. It takes me a while to say, "I'm sorry," and usually I have trouble believing I'm the one who needs to apologize.

If you know me well, you're probably not surprised. I take no pride in it though; it's a part of my character I'm working on. Maybe it's the Enneagram three in me, or the insatiable desire to seem like I have it all together. Whatever the cause, I've found that it's really difficult to be a good husband while also never thinking I am wrong. (Some of you are nodding your heads right now in agreement, others are shaking your head shaming me.)

I also don't like fighting. It's just the worst. Can't everyone just be happy all the time? Can't we just avoid conflict, or at least stuff it under some rock way down in our heart and pretend like everything is okay? I've been around so many marriages that were laced with shouting, slamming doors, driving away to cool off, then never fully resolving the conflict with an honest and humble conversation. I've seen dating relationships that seem to rise and fall weekly, sometimes daily. Like two warriors facing off on the front lines of a battle, both armed and dangerous, both ready to inflict wounds before wounds are received. It can get ugly. That's probably why I hate fighting so much.

Our first year of marriage was pretty stinking easy. I know that's not the story for everyone, but ours was care-free, drama-free, fight-free. We're both fairly easy-to-get-along-with people, so honestly, the first twelve months were blissful. The first few years were blissful, if I'm honest. We never fought. Rarely argued. Seldom disagreed. We just both went with the flow. And as the years rolled by, we both wondered what all the hype was about. Why did so many of our peers have a different story? And, what could ever lead to married people fighting? We both worked part-time jobs, watched Oprah on weekday afternoons, and cooked food in our small kitchen. All was good.

I don't recall what our first big fight was about. I was actually trying to remember when the first time was that Jamie and I had major conflict. It could have been the time I forgot to pay the electric bill. I was on tour, gone from home for about a month. I could have sworn I paid the bills before I left. But as soon as Jamie called me crying and yelling (yes, at the same time—there was a potent blend of sadness and anger), I knew I had in fact not paid the electric bill.

I held the phone about six inches from my face as I listened to her explain the grim situation at home. She and the kids had been out of town for a few days, and as she parked the car and hustled the kids toward the house, she instantly smelled an indescribably horrible smell seeping from the house. She said it smelled like a combination of rotting flesh and hot garbage, and when she opened the door to a completely unlit house she instantly knew the electricity had been shut off for a long time. So long, in fact, that everything in the freezer had not only thawed, but spoiled and turned to a sloppy, disgusting goo.

Now you understand why she was so mad. Now you understand the blend of sadness and anger. Anger that it was my fault. Sadness that she'd be the one to clean up the disgusting goo.

I don't know for sure if that was the first big fight, but it was a pretty big one. And, as much as I hated admitting I was wrong, in that moment, there was no one else to blame. No defense. No argument. I was the worst.

Throughout the years, we've fought about parenting styles, lack of communication, poor calendaring, over-extending ourselves, being selfish, how clean and organized the house should be, unrealistic expectations we both have for each other, and even silly things like whether or not the toilet seat should remain up after each use. (You can probably guess where I land on this complicated issue.)

Fighting isn't bad; it's necessary.

Somewhere along the way though, we've learned that fighting isn't bad; it's necessary. A marriage that doesn't have conflict isn't a marriage at all. So, to avoid conflict or run from it completely is actually moving *away* from a healthy marriage, not toward it.

But there's a difference between fighting *against* your spouse and fighting *with* your spouse.

It may seem like semantics, but when the heat turns up in any given moment, you have to make a crucial choice: *Will you view your spouse as the opponent you're trying to defeat, or the friend you're trying to win back? Will you treat your spouse like a person on the other team, or a person on the same team?*

Winning a friend is always better than beating an enemy. And, in marriage, it takes an incredible amount of work, patience, and humility to fight in a way where both parties win, forging not just resolve, but a deeper friendship.

"As iron sharpens iron, so a brother sharpens another" (Prov. 27:17 NIV), applies to marriage as well! When two pieces of iron strike each other, sparks and pieces of metal go flying everywhere. But through the conflict, they both become sharper.

Are you catching the difference here? At the end of the day, it's all about posture. It's not *don't fight*, it's *fight right*.

In every wartime scenario throughout the history of humanity, posture has mattered immensely. If two rivals come at each other with guns blazing, it usually doesn't end well. But if two opposing parties come with a willing posture—working together to understand, hear, and validate—peace is the tasty fruit that both can savor.

Have you ever wondered why we shake hands when we greet people? Perhaps you asked this question for the first time when coronavirus swept the globe, and for the first time in your life you weren't shaking hands. Normally, though, we do it all the time. Friends do it, politicians do it, strangers do it, even enemies have found a way to shake hands at the end of a tough conversation.

There have been thousands of variations on the handshake throughout time. In ancient history, people greeted each other by embracing the forearm or placing a hand on a shoulder. In more recent times we have fist bumps, high-fives, hugs, and the strange combo that my kids greet their friends with—the one I can never quite get right, and it makes me feel insecure and look completely stupid not knowing how to do it. (I've asked them to show me, but no matter how hard I try, I still get it wrong. I weirdly fumble it up, interdigitate the wrong fingers the wrong way, then walk away in shame looking like a moron to a bunch of teenagers.)

Regardless, there's something endearing about the handshake, no matter how it has evolved.

But where did the handshake come from? When did two rivals decide to shake hands as a sign of peace? I was surprised when I looked up where it came from. The history of the handshake gives us incredible insight into how much posture matters, especially when it comes to avoiding war with another human being. The handshake first showed up on the scene in Ancient Greece. When two people came together, potentially in conflict, or trying desperately to signify comradery and peace, they would shake right hands. It communicated something profound—I have no weapon in my hand. I come to you unarmed. I will not harm you. I come empty-handed. Here, I'll show you.

What if we approached fighting in the same way in our dating relationships and marriage? Imagine how much it could change not just the conversation, but the outcome if both people showed up on the scene without weapons. No ammunition. Nothing to inflict harm or wounds. Just an open hand and humble heart that says, "We need to talk about some things. This is gonna be hard for both of us. But, I have no weapon. You are not my enemy."

Okay, let's get honest. Here's a question for you to wrestle with as you read this. Typically in fighting, what is *your* weapon of choice? We all have a favorite weapon and ammunition to fire off at the spouse we're in conflict with. What are the ones you tend to pull out during wartime? What's holstered in your back pocket, loaded and ready when the time is just right?

Is it cutting the other person down with words? Is it silent treatment? Is it bringing up the past, the old sins of the other person? Is it anger and rage? Is it manipulation? Is it self-deprecation? Or is it just passive aggression, hoping that will be a Band-aid to a much bigger problem?

Mine is clear as day.

There's no mystery to what my weapon of choice is. I tend to use the power of words to convince Jamie that she is wrong and I am absolutely right. I don't yell. I've never slammed doors or stormed out of the house to drive to the local pub in anger. My weapon is far more subtle—I just have a way of using words for personal gain. Maybe I can blame the two years of studying Persuasion in college, but I can usually win a debate just by clever wording, whether I even believe my argument or not.

And there's just zero way for me to truly love, serve, and complement Jamie while holding that weapon. I've had to change. To take the weapon out of the arsenal.

So, check your hand. Hold it out. See your weapon of choice? It's probably different than mine, but it's still a dangerous one.

Listen, the best thing you could possibly do to love your spouse is to not only *refuse* to use that weapon, but to take it further—to ask God to completely obliterate it. It has to go. And He'd be happy to do that for you—even if the process is slow and painful.

I've come to this conclusion. I don't think you can truly have a happy marriage until you and your spouse have learned to fight appropriately. Resolving conflict in a timely, humble, self-aware kind of way actually produces a strange happiness as you draw closer to your spouse, not further away. The Bible tells us that we are to treat our spouse with love and never harshness. In Colossians 3:19, Paul tells husbands to love their wives in this way, and he doesn't qualify that command with "unless you are in a fight!"

So do this. Show up to a fight. But show up with empty hands. Let your spouse see that you come with nothing but a desire for unity, no matter the expense.

Let your spouse see that no weapon is needed. No one will be declared winner or loser at the end. It's just two people coming together, defenseless and without the aim to injure. Two pieces of iron coming together in conflict, talking candidly and honestly, and walking away in unity and more sharpened for the long journey of marriage.

Suzanne Stabile said it best in a recent conversation. "Aaron," she said to me, "it's darn near impossible to wound your spouse when conflict arises if you're talking knee to knee, hand in hand, eye to eye, unwilling to go to war against each other, but fighting *for* each other." I'll never forget that conversation. And, as uncomfortable as it is to fight or argue in that literal posture, it will absolutely change how you resolve conflict. It is darn near impossible to wound someone you're embracing with physical touch. She's right.

> I don't think you can truly have a happy marriage until you and your spouse have learned to fight appropriately.

Actually, Proverbs 27:17 says it even better than Suzanne did. "Iron sharpens iron, and one person sharpens another" (CSB). Be a sharpener, not a wounder. Be a refiner, but not a jerk. Be confrontational, but not without grace. Admit you're wrong, even when it hurts. That's a sharpened marriage. That's a happy friendship. That's a complementary marriage.

CHAPTER 7

Forgive

To win a battle with a sword or gun is a fairly small thing—it's easy if you think about it. But to win a battle God's way requires something much harder to come by this day and age.

You can't buy it at a store, you won't find it in a strategic plan for success, and very few people have stumbled across it throughout the generations. The most beautiful victory in any battle or conflict comes *only* with earnest forgiveness.

One of the most precious gifts you can give to your spouse is practicing the lost art and sacred mystery of forgiveness.

I don't know if it's possible to attend a wedding without hearing the beautiful words of 1 Corinthians 13 at some point in the ceremony. "Love is patient. Love is kind," begins the long address on how we are to show love not only to each other, but to the world. I'm convicted every single time I hear it, every time I read it. Sometimes when we've heard something so many times, it can lose its weight, but for some reason I've never become numb to those words.

They expose the kind of love I hope to have. I want to be known for those things. I want to love in those ways. My friendships, my marriage, my fathering, my pastoring, and my interaction with the world around me—I want them to read like that! And, if you stop and think about it, you probably do too. The desire is in you— somewhere. You were created in the image of God. You have His fingerprints all over you, and this is the kind of person He made you to become. So there's a yearning inside you—a mysterious one—to be this kind of person. And although this passage wasn't originally intended to address marriage, I'm so glad we use that scripture as the template for what we're aiming for in a covenant with a spouse.

There are a few aspects of loving someone, though, that are more difficult to practice than others. It may be fairly easy for you to be kind, or to place trust in a spouse. It may be fairly natural for you to honor him or her, to build them up without tearing them down. But there's a good chance that every single one of us has difficulty with one aspect of loving—forgiveness. Or as 1 Corinthians so eloquently puts it, "keeping no record of wrong."

If everything everyone had ever done to wrong us were written down on paper, it'd hardly fit into a few Moleskine journals. We've all been wronged. The pages are too many to count. We've all been wounded or sinned against. But we have a real choice in what we're going to do with those things, and how we're going to respond to the people who did them.

We can stack up the journals neatly on the memory shelves of our brain, flipping through them when the time seems right. We can highlight them, underline them, memorize them, take them to heart, and let those memories eat up our soul. But this approach has some unintended consequences. Soon enough, the words become larger than life, villainizing not just the person who said or did them to us, but turning us into a new villain ready to seek out vengeance, an eye-for-an-eye. Eventually the grudge we've held against others so hardens our hearts that we become just as much of a monster as we perceive the other party to be.

Or, we can do what the scripture says. We can throw them out. Take them off the shelf. Throw them in the burn pile. Keep no record of those wrongs.

"I can *forgive* her, but I'll never *forget* what she did." I've heard this many times while counseling couples, either in a dating season or marriage. It's a tough phrase to hear, maybe tougher to unravel. It's human instinct to store up those wrongdoings, and so hard to truly "keep no record." In fact, as I'm writing this, I can recall how many times in previous chapters I've brought up things people have said to me that have hurt me (chapter 4 as an example), and I'm even convicted of not only keeping a record of those wrongdoings, but also writing them down for you to now read. It seems impossible to dump all those journals into a fire, watch the embers float into the cool sky, then walk away, doesn't it?

I'm not a neurologist, so I can't speak to this in a medical sense, but I don't know if we are actually capable of choosing to forget some of those things. There are things done to you that you'll never be able to forget. But I do know it's possible to not hold those things tightly, to not give them power anymore, and to forgive that person freely and generously, shutting the Moleskines permanently.

In marriage, you'll have to forgive. And you'll have to forgive often. Whether it's sexual sin, words said to you, spiritual failures, or just not meeting expectations—forgiveness is the only way forward. I'll dare to say this: you'll have to forgive your spouse in more ways and more times than they deserve. The only way to practice that sort of earnest and sincere forgiveness is to truly embrace how you have been forgiven—completely—by a holy and perfect God.

Ephesians 4:32 is probably one of the most convicting verses on forgiveness in the whole Bible. "Be kind to one another, tenderhearted, forgiving one another."

It's a command, not an option. It's the Word of God telling you and I how we *are* to live, not merely suggesting one good option we should consider. Most of us can wrap our hands around "being kind to one another," but it seems like it ramps up quite a bit to add tenderheartedness to the mix. That's altogether deeper than kindness. Tenderheartedness is not just about showing kindness; it requires an alteration to the heart. You can *show* kindness to someone in a moment without *being* tenderhearted toward them. So it's next level to say, "God keep my heart tender, always sensitive, always compassionate, forever moved toward love." That's more than a single act of kindness.

But, if *showing* kindness and *being* tenderhearted isn't bold enough, the verse adds a much more difficult third command—"forgiving one another." There it is. Show kindness, be tenderhearted, and no matter how hard it may be, always be willing to forgive anyone who has wronged you.

We can't get away from it, can't delete it from Scripture, can't gloss over it. It's there. It's a command. But with a hard command comes a gentle reminder of *how* we are to do this. It's in the next phrase I haven't mentioned yet.

"Be kind to one another, tenderhearted, forgiving one another, as God in Christ forgave you."

> The *only* way to have a forgiving heart is to realize the depth of forgiveness we have received from God through Jesus Christ.

There's the how. The *only* way to have a forgiving heart is to realize the depth of forgiveness we have received from God through Jesus Christ.

Christian, do you realize how fiercely and

fully God has forgiven you through Jesus? From the biggest things in your life, to the smallest daily failures, you are forgiven. There's not one ounce of record being held against you. Jesus took all the journals filled with your filthy past, your checkered present, and your uncertain future, and burned them up when He took every sin to the cross two thousand years ago. There are no pages left. No scribbled notes with burnt edges litter the dust beneath the cross of Christ. Look hard enough and you can't even find a scrap of paper with a single letter on it. They're gone. Forever. All of your wrongdoings completely forgotten, forever turned into unreadable ash. You are completely and wholly forgiven.

For some, this resounds with the beauty of a heavenly symphony. You can't not hear the power of forgiveness reverberating in the bones of your chest, because you know how great your sin was. You can recall the things you've done, and how terrible they were. You can hardly take in the overwhelming joy of knowing all your sins, *even those unspeakable ones*, have been forgiven.

For others, this doesn't feel that big. Maybe you don't have a story of what most would consider great sin. You grew up in church, you did mostly right things, and so it may be tempting for you to think, *I mean, I haven't really wronged God that much.*

And for some, you still have a hard time believing it all. It seems too good to be true. Yes, you affirm that Jesus' life and death and resurrection washed you clean, but you live in the guilt and shame that you still carry, not quite able to see yourself as God sees you.

We've all sinned. We've all fallen short. Jesus often spoke of His flattened-out view of sin. There is no "big" sin and there is no "small" sin. Some have actually committed adultery, but Jesus flattened out adultery by saying even if you think about someone who is not your spouse in a sexual way, you've committed adultery in your heart. Sin is sin. Without degree, without a label of bigness or smallness. Through the holy eyes of Jesus, all sin separated us from God.

So, we're all on the same playing field. You've sinned. I've sinned. She's sinned. He's sinned. But the good news is that for those who have faith in Christ, the healing balm of His forgiveness has made every record of those sins vanish. That's how much you've been forgiven. That's how deep God's well of forgiveness goes. Beyond human understanding, but not beyond what humanity is called to believe and practice.

You are called to practice forgiveness, as God in Christ forgave you. You're called to have a deep well of forgiveness, just like His. A well that doesn't run dry or exhaust itself. A well that continually pours out to those around you. A well that continually pours out to your spouse or future spouse. That's the high calling. That's the hard command.

So, how do you do that? How do you forgive your spouse, especially when some of the things you may have to forgive them for seem unforgivable?

You have one option. You look to Jesus.

See the kindness with which He has pursued you, loved you, served you. See His tender heart, full of compassion, full of empathy, full of affection for you. See His mighty act of forgiveness, swift, once and for all—where He who knew no sin became sin, your sin. Then willfully took your sin to a cross where He shed His blood and let His life extinguish, forever sealing this statement over your precious life: *I love you. It is finished.*

Oh, you have been forgiven. See Jesus! As you walk away from that scene, be kind to one another. Let your heart remain tenderized. God in Christ set fire to your wrongdoings and remembered them no more. Go and do likewise.

CHAPTER 8

Sex

The only thing worse than watching a sex education film in middle school is watching a *Christian* sex education film in Sunday school.

I can still remember the awkwardness of the fifty-year-old Sunday school teacher at our little Independent Baptist church as he pushed play on the VCR, poured more coffee into his Styrofoam cup, and sat in a folding chair in the back corner of the room. I'm pretty sure he was sweating more than I was as the cheesy 1980s video began.

The content of that video was nothing like you're imagining. It really was just a couple of old married people talking about abstinence. Weird, terrible, bad acting, and even worse music. As I nervously sat slumped in an old, plaid couch next to five other middle school boys in a run-down student ministry room tucked in the back corner of the church fellowship hall, a few thoughts raced through my head.

One, sex is very bad.

Two, sex cannot be discussed without it being strangely uncomfortable.

Three, Christians only have sex to make babies.

As the forty-five-minute film finally came to an end, the teacher stood up, turned the lights on, (side note: sex education films should always be shown with all the lights on; darkness just makes it feel even more creepy) and said, "Okay. Anyone have a question?"

I'm sure you're just shocked to hear that no one had questions—or at least we didn't dare ask. The main question I had was, "Can we please *never* do this again?!"

In all reality, my mind was plagued with so many unanswered questions for many, many years. When I saw movies, sex (although it was only hinted at) seemed to be the ultimate experience for any couple to embark upon. It seemed thrilling, like the big finale in a good rom com.

When I watched pornography, sex was clearly portrayed as something that everyone wants all the time, and will do whatever is necessary to get.

When I heard friends in high school and college talk about sex, it sounded like the most possible fun anyone could ever have. And if you weren't having it, you were less than a person. So you either joined the conversation and faked it, or just walked away feeling embarrassed that you hadn't stumbled into one of the great experiences in life that all your peers had.

But when it came to Christians talking about sex, it always seemed dirty. Something to avoid at all times. Even when people spoke of sex in the context of marriage, it seemed to be utilitarian, just something you do every once in a while, with nothing but mystery and silence covering every conversation about it.

Everything I ever learned about sex in my years of growing up came from what I watched online.

So I couldn't truly learn about sex from Christians. And I didn't learn much about sex from public education. I certainly didn't hear about it from my parents. Where did all of my knowledge about sex come from?

Pornography.

Everything I ever learned about sex in my years of growing up came from what I watched online. And sadly, this is far too common in our culture, just like it was when dial-up internet opened new and dangerous horizons for me as a fourteen-year-old boy.

Maybe that's your story, too.

Pornography has had a profound and negative effect on how our culture views sex. It has replaced the reality of sex with a fantasy—one that is distorted and twisted. And when we build our worldview on something distorted and twisted, it's hard to unwind that from our human relationships—even if we are following after Jesus and trying to do it the right way.

In pornography, sex revolves around doing whatever it takes to get what will satisfy you. From a man's perspective, sex in pornography is about conquering, dominating, while from the woman's perspective, it's about manipulating and enticing the other person to get what she wants. Porn essentially is a brutal and wicked answer to the question, *How can I get what I want?*

There's no secret about the fact that porn is the largest entertainment industry in the world. In 2020, porn sites got more traffic than Netflix, Amazon, and Instagram *combined*. And it's not even hidden anymore.

Plastic sealed magazines in the back of a convenient store have been traded for city billboards and social media ads, normalizing porn into something that just feels common. In many ways, porn websites have become like showing up to a giant buffet. You can find whatever you want. It's a pick-and-choose sort of mentality when viewing pornography. And we all know that nothing is "enough" for us.

As a former porn addict, I can tell you point blank—nothing was enough. You only want more, and more and more. And since God freed me from the addiction to pornography in my later college years, I've come to terms with how formative that was for me.

Now, this whole chapter isn't meant to be a deep-dive into the dangers and effects of pornography, but I tell you all of that to remind you of this—the worst part about porn isn't what you see, but what it teaches you.

Too many single men and women have all kinds of misconceptions about what sex will be if and when marriage is in the cards for them. Too many married people struggle and argue about sex. She wants it more than he does, or vice versa. Did you know that the two main reasons that marriages fall apart, or struggle are money and sex? It's staggering to think about how complex and nuanced sex can be within the context of marriage, but unless we have a healthy, godly framework for sex in marriage, we'll always struggle.

Although our current culture is over-sexualized, sex is not something we invented or discovered. It was part of God's original and good design for how a marriage should function. Sure, sex is necessary for creating kids, but that's not the primary reason God invented the thing. It's also supposed to be thrilling and fun in a marriage, but that's not why He came up with the idea either.

Ephesians 5:31 sheds some helpful light on the mystery of sex.

> For this reason, a man will leave his
> father and mother and be united to his
> wife, and the two will become one flesh.

There is a one-flesh-ness that is accomplished when a married couple forges their marriage, sealing it with a covenant, and engaging in sex. That's why sex can be so detrimental to both people outside the context of marriage. There is no such thing as "casual sex." If you have a history of sex outside of or prior to marriage, you know this really well. You become one with the person you have sex with. There's more than attraction, there's bonding that happens. Heart and soul connect in the deepest of ways, and whether we want to admit it or not, sex binds people in a way that nothing else does. Sex says, "You get all of me. I'm not holding anything back. We belong to each other."

Now, if you've messed up—either in singleness or marriage—you need to hear that there's nothing God can't heal, nothing He won't forgive, and nothing He can't bring freedom to. Trust that! He loves you, and can turn even the most broken story into something beautiful. Just like I said in the last chapter, there is no one big sin that's worse than all the others—sexual sin certainly isn't the exception.

But sex—and sexual sin—is still serious, and we should treat it seriously. So, there are a couple of things I want to address. Some from my own experience, others from pastoring countless singles and married people along the way. If I only get to tell you a few things about sex, these are the things I'd want to highlight.

1. Sex is not a dirty three-letter word.

According to the Bible, God created sex for marriage between a man and a woman. And when He created it,

He didn't make it something dirty or worldly. While the world has twisted it into something He didn't intend, it's actually something He thought up during the creation event. We didn't stumble into it, He made it. And God doesn't make dirty things. If anyone has ever told you that sex is bad—a pastor, a parent, a leader—don't listen to them! There are actually long sections of Scripture (you should read Song of Solomon someday) that celebrate sex, affirm pleasure within marriage, and highlight that it is good and right for couples to be passionately in love.

First Corinthians 7 shows that God doesn't just "allow" for sex in a marriage, He actually tells us to do it. God knows that it is good and right, and some of us need to be freed up to not view a thrilling sex life as something bad, or something that is only reserved for people who don't follow Jesus. You can't read the Bible and come away with any belief that God doesn't want marriages to be marked with passion and sex. When the Bible restricts sex, it's not because it's dirty. The Bible reserves sex for marriage because it is *so* good and beautiful that you should reserve it only for your spouse.

2. Sex is not the ultimate; relationship is.

I already mentioned that our culture is way over-sexualized. You almost can't get away from sex these days. It's the main theme of advertising and marketing, it's in every movie and story, and in many ways we've exaggerated it to be the ultimate human experience. In doing so, we've made abstinence seem archaic and ridiculous.

Most single friends I know who are following Jesus have decided to buy into the biblical ethic of celibacy. Many believing friends who are same-sex attracted have made a life-time commitment to abstaining from sex. And you know what? They have to keep reminding themselves that they aren't less human, or missing out on the ultimate experience in life—*because they are not*. Sex is not the ultimate thing; *relationship* is. And I know hundreds of singles who are happy, fulfilled, vibrant, and deeply connected in their relationships with God and others. Without sex.

One of my best friends is a single dude who follows Jesus. He said something to me that he truly meant, and I was so blown away by this: "Singleness isn't a curse. I've actually found it to be a blessing, because for however

long I'm single, I know that Jesus can be my one mag-
nificent obsession."

Wow. That's it. If you're single, maybe you need to
highlight that, underline it, tattoo it on your arm. We
were created to be in relationship. With God and with
others. And sex is not the magic ingredient to the equa-
tion of being loved that makes it all work.

Jesus is the most authentic human being to ever
live—the most complete, fulfilled, joyful person ever.
And He did it all without ever being married, without
ever having sex. Sam Alberry writes, "The moment
we claim a life of celibacy to be dehumanizing, we are
implying that Jesus himself is only subhuman."[2] But Jesus
is not subhuman; He is the truest, most perfect human.
Our Savior was a single man in His early thirties.

This is also important to remember for married
couples that, for whatever reason, aren't able to have sex.
Maybe there is a health condition or circumstance pre-
venting sex—either for a season or for life. That does not
have to ruin a marriage, because sex is not ultimate.

---

[2] Sam Allberry, *7 Myths about Singleness* (Wheaton, IL:
Crossway, 2019), 25.

Listen, you were created to be in relationship, with or without sex in the picture. So, aim for that. And if for whatever reason God has marriage in your story, then experience sex within the bounds of the ultimate human experience—relationship.

3. Sex has boundaries.

I've already said it, but biblical sex is reserved for a man and a woman in a covenantal marriage. But what about within that marriage? Are there boundaries?

I love honest people. People who aren't afraid to ask questions, no matter how hard or potentially awkward. A good friend sheepishly asked, "Is oral sex okay in a Christian marriage?" It's a question among many that we don't ask very often out loud. But maybe we should be more open about real questions like this. "Is it okay to watch porn together as a married couple?" "Is it dirty to use foreplay?" "Is there *anything* out of bounds??"

My answer is always the same. Start with this: "Is the action in and of itself sinful? Does it cause you or your spouse or anyone else to sin?" If the answer is *yes*, it's not something God would want you to do. The question of whether or not a Christian couple should watch porn together is a resounding, "no." You can't watch porn without lusting after a person that you're not married to. Watching two people engaging in sin should not arouse you; it should cause you to grieve.

But if something isn't sinful, then what? I think you ask this next: "Is this beneficial and comfortable for both people involved?" Some people have a tragic history with sexual sin, so there will be more boundaries in sex that will be beneficial and make the other person feel more loved. You just need to talk through it and be incredibly candid. Sex is never meant to be something that degrades, demoralizes, or makes one of the two feel objectified or worthless. If anything, sex is meant to serve the other person—not, "what can I get out of this?" but, "what can I give to make sure the other person feels loved, valued, seen, and cared for?"

4. Sex isn't about "What can I get?" but, "What can I give?"

First Corinthians 7 makes this point really clear. Each person in the marriage shouldn't be concerned with getting the pleasure they want, but instead giving the pleasure the other person wants. It sounds one-sided when you read it, but if both people are practicing this mind-set, the result is a vibrant sex life, and a closer intimacy with your spouse.

5. Sex in marriage is the fruit of deep friendship.

Sex does not equal love, and love does not equal sex. However, a healthy biblical sex life in marriage is the fruit of deep friendship. I can't tell you how many marriages I know that have become dull and boring, completely void of romance. It makes me sad, but I get it. Unless you're striving to stay romantic, it can just become casual and apathetic. I was talking to Jamie about this chapter, and was reminded how much harder it is to stay romantic when you've both got really busy jobs, and four teenagers, and two dogs, and bills, and schedules, and things constantly breaking around the house. The thrill and romance of dating can seriously numb as life gets busier and busier. But, we're never meant to have marriage without romance.

So, how is it lost?

When you're dating—as a Christian who is reserving sex for marriage—all you have is romance. It's like there's a giant wall up that you can't climb over. You can't have sex yet, so romance is all you got! You text, call, date, and can't wait to be around each other. But when that wall is suddenly removed, marriage is sealed, and everything is now available in sex, the romance is one of the first things to go.

It's like waiting years to get a reservation at one of the best restaurants in the world. (I know because I've done this.) There's a date on the calendar, and when it finally arrives you get to enjoy the greatest meal of your life. But if you were able to have that meal every single day of your life, it would slowly lose its charm. You'd start to crave Whataburger every once in a while, while the world's greatest chef stands right in front of you with a 5-star meal. The "romance" of that experience fades as you're able to access it anytime you want.

That's why we have to fight for romance in marriage, especially as the years roll by.

For nearly twenty years, Jamie and I have been consistent to date each other. We have a weekly date night, we try to write letters to each other, we kiss in the kitchen, and hold hands on walks. We are best friends. We really like each other. But it takes work to keep the romance going. I don't ever want to become numb to her, never view her as the world's greatest restaurant that I'm suddenly bored with.

And you know what happens when you stay romantic? Sex is better. It's just that simple.

6. Sex ultimately points to the gospel.

I know how weird that sounds. But it's true.

There's something here we need to wrestle with as we strive toward viewing sex in the right way as Christians. Of course it's fun, is meant to be enjoyed, and it's something we grow into as we continue through years and years of marriage. But it's not only a gift from God, it also has a glorious *significance*.

Tim Keller gives helpful insight to this significance:

> Sex is sacred because it is the analogy of the joyous self-giving and pleasure of love within the life of the Trinity. The Father, Son, and Holy Spirit live in a relationship of glorious devotion to each other, pouring love and joy into one another continually. Sex between a man and a woman points to the love

of the Trinity, as well as that between
Christ and the believer.[3]

In the same way that Christ loves the bride (the church) and gave His life for her, and the bride loves Jesus and surrenders everything to Him—this is the picture of sex in a marriage. The one-flesh-ness of marriage is expressed in sex, just like the one-flesh-ness of our relationship to Christ is expressed in an unbreakable, intimate, never-ending, fully committed romance that we have with God. Sex is meant to be a living picture of the vibrant, unshakable, everlasting love that Christ has with the believer. It's meant to be wonderful because it mirrors something so wonderful!

Our view of sex—either in singleness or marriage—tells a lot about what we believe about God. He gave all of Himself to us through the love and work of Jesus, and He asks us to do the same in return—give all of ourselves to Him, unconditionally. While we are single, *and* if we are married. He offers the ultimate intimacy, without

---

[3] "The Gospel and Sex" found at http://208.106.253.109 /essays/the-gospel-and-sex.aspx and also at https://www .christ2rculture.com/resources/Ministry-Blog/The-Gospel -and-Sex-by-Tim-Keller.pdf.

limitations, and sealed with a promise to give us that intimate relationship indefinitely. There's no expiration date to His love and friendship.

The same is meant to be true in marriage. We offer ourselves to each other, intimately and freely, without any expiration date or hesitation. That's how sex in marriage is meant to be! To remind *us* of the gospel, and ultimately illustrate to the world around us—this is what our God is like.

> Sex is meant to be a living picture of the vibrant, unshakable, everlasting love that Christ has with the believer.

CHAPTER 9

Parent

Dad, can I ask you a serious question?" one of my sons asked timidly during his elementary school days.

We've always had an open-to-any-question kind of culture in our home. No question is too hard, too weird, or off-limits.

"Of course. What's up?" I asked, plopping on the couch next to him.

"Well . . ." he stuttered, "there's a word that I heard at school, and I don't know what it means. Everybody says it, and it seems like everyone knows what it is, so I just nod along like I know what they're talking about, but I don't."

I obviously braced for the worst. A body part. A terrible curse word. Something the kids were saying that *I* hadn't even heard.

"So . . . The word . . ." he fumbled to get it out.

"You can ask me anything, bro!" I said, leaning toward him in anticipation.

"So . . . the word is Pop-Tart. Dad, what is a Pop-Tart?"

In that moment a sigh of relief and a snicker of failure came over me. *I failed you! I thought. How could my own son not know what a Pop-Tart was.* In our attempt to eat healthy, clean food and rid our little house of junk food, I realized I had robbed him of one of life's greatest treasures—a crispy tart filled with strawberry syrup and covered in a delicious sugary icing. I pulled him from the couch, started the car, and said, "Son, I'm about to blow your mind."

After a quick trip to the nearby grocery store, I took him to the Pop-Tart aisle, stretched out my arm to the twenty-foot section of sugary goodness, and said, "Son, this is a Pop-Tart." We bought at least ten different flavors, then drove home, fired up the toaster, and all the mysteries of his seven-year-old life had finally been unlocked as he placed a steaming rectangle of fake sugar and processed dough into his mouth, while his body shook with absolute excitement.

Little did I realize that parenting would be marked by little failures along the way, and hiding the goodness of Pop-Tarts would be the smallest of them all.

Truth is, parenting is incredibly hard. There's no manual for how to train up your child, especially in the deeper things of life—the things that set the course for them to become whole and God-centered adults. Sometimes it feels a bit like you're swimming in the ocean, riding a fun wave here and there, but most of the time just paddling as hard as you can to not mess something up.

Questions like, "What's a Pop-Tart?" have turned into, "Why is there racism?" and "Why are some of my friends already having sex?" We've had to walk through the hard realities of life—injustice around the world, when to allow social media, how to parent in a culture where their minds

> Parenting is incredibly hard.

are always the target of every worldview and every advertiser, and an American culture that highlights success over character. Sometimes, I wish we were still explaining Pop-Tarts, but that world has morphed into a scarier one, a more real one, where the stakes are higher, and their love for Jesus is always under attack.

One of the things I'm so thankful for is that Jamie and I complement each other in parenting. I can't do it alone, and neither can she. Nor should we ever think we're doing it alone. We need each other, our kids need both of us. They need a strong, loving father—and they need a strong, loving mother. And one of the best things we can do as we parent our four children is to stay unified. We need to have our sights set on the same target. A splintered family unit—one where mom and dad are on two different pages—is a confusing one, and children are usually the ones who suffer most.

It's been helpful to have some values that we both focus on as we strive to be good parents. Jamie and I are obviously wired very different. She likes rules and Google Docs; I like fun and spontaneity. She wants their chores done each day; I want everyone to sleep as late as they want and stay up as late as they can. But for us to be unified in parenting, we have to come together. I have to care not just about the things I care about, but about the things Jamie cares about. Because, let's be honest, if I were solo parenting, the house would be a wreck, no one would have clean underwear, and schoolwork would never be a priority. Likewise, if she were solo parenting, she'd always be the heavy hand, and that's not fair to her or them.

Sometimes it's easy to think you're just parenting children. But this vision is too small. We're not just parenting children; we're shepherding children into adults.

We, of course, want obedient toddlers. We want compliant little boys and girls. We want teenagers who work hard. But while those things are all important, we have to have a wider vision than just the season of life they happen to be in at any moment. We aren't parenting children. We're raising adults.

Jamie and I have been entrusted for a brief amount of time to help shepherd them into adulthood. To give them the tools, resources, knowledge, experience, and upbringing that catapults them into leaving our home and being an adult who loves Jesus,

> We aren't parenting children. We're raising adults.

loves people, and is humbly confident in who God made them. And, if we miss that, we're just sending children out into the world. And we all know, we need less child-adults. We need more kind, humble, peace-making,

justice-seeking, creative, brilliant, loving adults who see
their role in the world as shining the spotlight on the
person and work of Jesus.

That's what we're aiming for.

That means Jamie and I have to be unified parents
shepherding our children into Christlike adults.

We have a family in our life that does this really well.
They are ten years ahead of us in terms of age and season
of life. Their kids are in their mid-twenties, and we for-
tunately had the privilege of watching them closely over
the past decade. We've seen them transition kids into
middle school, cheer on their high school graduates, celebrate a few of their kids' weddings, and basically have
a front-row seat to them doing their best to shepherd
their kids into adulthood. The entire time they've done
it with a Jesus focus. What a gift to get to watch them do
it, learn from their mistakes, then do our best to follow
their example.

So how do we do it? How do we shepherd our children into Christlike adults? I wish it was as easy as giving
you a few sentences or bullet points. I wish there was a
perfect instruction manual, keeping us from ever making a mistake along the way. But I've learned that escap-
ing mistakes isn't possible, and God uses those mistakes

to show our kids how much better Jesus is than Aaron and Jamie Ivey.

For our kids to actually see Jesus, we have to keep getting out of the way. I never want them to have a faulty view of their dad, thinking that I'm perfect, or only showing them the best parts of me so they'll believe I've got it all together. In fact, the more they see me confess and repent, the more they see my need for Jesus. And the more they see *my* need for Jesus, the more they'll see *their* need for Jesus. I never want to be an idol in their life. I don't want to present a false view of their dad, then one day down the road destroy them by messing up and showing them I'm actually a mess but was just too afraid to show them along the way. That wouldn't be helpful. But what *is* helpful is for my children to see me continually submitting myself to Jesus, continually admitting my need for Him, continually bringing my life to the altar, laying down myself because I truly believe Jesus is better.

That's the primary way I can lead them into adulthood—showing them that a true man of God is humble, honest, and vulnerable with his brokenness, and he will sacrifice and risk anything to follow and obey Jesus.

We also keep their adulthood at the forefront of our conversation. Not to scare them, but to give them a realistic perspective that their middle school and high school years are only temporary. We want them to savor each moment, but also be aimed at the future. I've found it helpful to ask a lot of questions. "What kind of man do you want to become?" "What kind of woman do you hope to be in twenty years?" We look at the current realities of their lives and help them see that every decision they are making today is setting the course for what kind of human they'll be ten years from now.

It's this forward-thinking, forward-speaking kind of parenting that reminds my kids that I actually am more concerned with who they will become than I am about who they currently are. Why? Because life is one massive journey toward heaven. And how easy it is to let parenting get tangled up only in the present moment, forgetting that our babies become leaders and fathers and mothers and presidents and plumbers. Let's set them up for that by giving them a big perspective on how much God loves them and wants to use them for His glory!

How do Jamie and I stay unified along the way? I mean, the forward focus is good and all, but our kids have two *very* different parents. We think differently, talk differently, view the world differently, and obviously would parent very differently if we weren't synced up.

First, we keep the main things the priority, and let the secondary things be secondary. What's most important? Is it important that our children accomplish all their tasks, homework, chores? Yes, it's important. But it will always be secondary to character. Someone who simply checks tasks off a list, yet has a hardened heart, or a prideful spirit, is not the kind of adult we want to send into the world.

Is it important that our kids are in the Word, a part of student ministry at church, learning how to pray, etc.? Yes, it's important. But it's secondary. What's most important is that they begin to develop a genuine love for the Lord. We all know it's easy to attend church events without having a heart that beats for Jesus. So, we take it slowly. We don't push things on them. Rather, we nudge them toward the heart of Jesus. Because the closer they get to the heart of Jesus, the more they'll want to give Him their whole life.

Is it important that they get an education, go to school, discover a career? Yes, it's important to be able to find your craft and provide for yourself. But what's more important? Discovering that you're wonderfully and perfectly made *by* God and *for* God. When a child discovers they are created *for* God, it doesn't matter what their career is, they won't be able to help but jump all-in, growing, maturing, developing into a strong woman or man of God who does whatever they do for the glory of God.

Is it important that they obey? Sure—but more important that they develop a heart that wants to obey God first. After that, it's easier to want to obey your authorities, whether it's a boss, a parent, or a teacher.

Is it important that they have a thrilling, happy childhood? Yes, but not at the cost of a realization that the world is broken, and most of the world lives in poverty or dire situations.

I guess what I'm saying is that Jamie and I lay down some of our personal preferences of parenting, because we want to be unified in the big picture. And the big picture means we have to zoom out to seeing them as future men and women of God. And that requires us locking arms, agreeing on the priorities, affirming them, fighting for them, and doing whatever possible to stay focused on parenting the future adults we see inside our children. For us, those priorities are shaping our kids' character, nudging them toward a genuine love for Jesus, helping them see the centrality and glory of God in their lives, teaching them to obey God, and giving them an honest picture of the world. We figure the rest can fall in line.

It's kind of like what Jesus said in the gospel of Matthew: "Seek first the kingdom of God and his righteousness, and all these things will be provided for you" (Matt. 6:33 csb). We want to help our children become adults who seek first God's kingdom and righteousness; the rest will take care of itself.

CHAPTER 10

Mission

I've been a fan of art for as long as I can remember. It has the unique ability to capture one's attention, to stir the senses, to break up the monotony of life, to remind you that there's always something beautiful out there waiting to be seen.

I grew up in West Texas. If you've never been to Marfa, Texas, or hiked the heights of Big Bend National Park, you're missing out. The landscape alone is enough to make you believe that God is the best Artist there is. Not to mention the stars at night. If you stand in the middle of the West Texas desert at night, you'll look up to see a billion tiny lights busting through the black blanket above, and you can't help but stand in awe.

My father loved painting landscapes of West Texas while we lived there. And, to be honest, he's a phenomenal painter. His skillset is in a genre called photo-realism, the kind of paintings that look stunningly like real life. When he finishes a painting, most people swear it's a photograph. Whether it's a painting of an animal, a Texas sunset, or a portrait of a loved one, they all look incredibly real. I remember watching him work for hours on a painting, sometimes months, painting the smallest of details, skinny lines, droopy curves, then bring color and shade to the tone of human skin, or the texture of tree bark.

He rarely paints anything that hasn't stolen his heart in the first place. You can try to commission him to paint a portrait of your grandmother or family Christmas photo, but he won't do it unless his heart is somehow moved by the story. He can't help but want to only paint things that stir his emotions. So it's always been easy for him to paint the vast West Texas mountain ranges, or the hills of East Tennessee. I think that's what makes a good painter, and a good painting, so different than just a photograph or a photocopy.

A good painting gives you a glimpse into the artist's heart, not just the subject he or she is painting. And when you gaze with delight on a great painting, you can understand the artist more, and be inspired by how much beauty there truly is in the world.

I want you to know today, that this is what God has in mind for your marriage. Your marriage has the uncanny and unique ability to be a living painting that the world gets to look at with delight. And when people look at it, they are meant to see just how good God is.

This is the reality of marriage that we don't typically think about. Too often we only highlight marriage as a commitment—rings on fingers, vows confessed, promises made. And while marriage contains an essence of commitment, it's not simply an agreement between two willing parties.

Other times, marriage is only viewed as something archaic, something for an older generation, something too idealistic, not attainable in today's context.

Perhaps the most common view of marriage is that it primarily benefits the couple, and no one else. We often idolize marriage into being the most epic thing any human can enjoy. That picture of marriage is couple-centric; it doesn't leave room for how life-giving marriage should be to those around the couple.

I want you to see that marriage is much more profoundly purposeful than any of those misconceptions.

Marriage is a living portrait God has painted to show the world His goodness.

Simply put, marriage is mission. Its purpose is to show the world God's covenantal, unbreakable, unstoppable, unending love. That is the nature of marriage, and it's the purpose of every marriage—yours and mine.

God, the masterful artist, takes a blank canvas, then through your story and your spouse's story, puts Himself on display—much like a treasured painting on display in a museum. It's not only there for every onlooker to enjoy, but to give a glimpse into the heart of the painter.

Your marriage is meant to be one of your greatest forms of mission to the world around you.

Let me tell you how this unfolds for Jamie and me.

We love having people around us. We love hospitality. Having people in our home is one of our favorite things. To look around our dining room table and see fifteen people laughing, talking, and eating good food absolutely thrills us. We recently had a wedding in our backyard, and both Jamie and

> Marriage is a living portrait God has painted to show the world His goodness.

I got teary as we stood with a bunch of twenty-year-olds that we love, *all* in our lives for a reason, for a purpose. We love having deep conversations in our kitchen with singles, helping them navigate through the complexities of following Jesus, dating if it comes, and giving their lives away for the sake of the gospel. We find ourselves hosting our middle school and high school kids' friend groups, and see it as an incredible privilege to be able to show them a healthy family—not a perfect one, but one that loves and loves and loves.

Our marriage has become one of our greatest forms of ministry.

You know, Jamie and I have two very different jobs. She's a podcaster, runs a company, and uses words to preach the good news of Jesus all over the world. I am a pastor, I lead and develop creative people, and use songs and melodies to preach the good news of Jesus all over the world. People often ask us, "How do you do two totally different jobs or ministries and stay unified?" It always catches us off guard a little bit.

Honestly, we *don't* have two totally different ministries. Sure, we have different careers—as I'm sure you and your spouse fill your days with very different activities. But Jamie and I have always had ONE mission. Our mission is simple: Love God, and tell everyone we can how good He is.

And how do we find ourselves doing that? By showing up. Showing up to anything and everything that is in front of us. With the mess, with the chaos, with honesty, and with a confidence in this: Our marriage is meant to be a living picture to the world around us that *God is good.*

See, you don't have to have a perfect marriage to do that. We don't! Because when people see your flaws and your failures, if you're living on mission, they end up seeing God, not you. They see a couple that isn't perfect but still surrenders themselves to God. They see God using brokenness for good things. The painting communicates, *Wow, God loves flawed people.*

> Our mission is simple: Love God, and tell everyone we can how good He is.

If you're killing it right now, firing on all cylinders, and living on mission as best as you can, great. People will end up seeing God, not you. They see a couple that has been fueled by grace, and still gives the credit to

God, alone. The painting communicates, *Wow, God can change people.*

Paintings are never perfect. But the best ones—the most stunning ones—are honest.

I want you to hear today that your marriage is bigger than you. It's meant for more than you. It's meant to be used as a powerful way of communicating to the world just how good God is. It may sound churchy, but it's still true—your marriage is meant to put on display the gospel.

Why do I have this view of marriage? Why am I so convinced that marriage is such a unique opportunity to display God's goodness, a canvas for Him to show the world His love? Well, because God tells us that very thing. He tells us that marriage was created to paint a picture of the gospel—the good news about Jesus' life, death, and resurrection to bring broken and sinful people like us into a relationship of love and joy with God. I think God can use singleness to display that He is more than enough, and I think He can use marriage to display His unending commitment and faithfulness.

It's not that Jesus' relationship with us is a picture of marriage; it's that marriage was created to be a picture of Jesus' relationship with us.

One of the authors in the New Testament was commenting on a very old passage of Scripture from earlier in the Bible that says that in marriage, a husband and wife "become one flesh." This author, Paul, called that a mystery. "This mystery is profound," he said, "but I am talking about Christ and the church" (Eph. 5:32 csb). Your marriage is a display of God's goodness and the gospel because it is a picture of Jesus and His love for His people.

I wonder what would change if we began to view marriage this way? Not just as something good for the couple, but a blessing from God for a whole community. Of course, when marriage is working properly, the way God intended it, you'll enjoy it plenty too. It will be amazing. But, it will also spill out to every person around you, blessing more people than you thought possible.

Strangers will be awestruck as they see an honest, loving couple following Jesus.

Singles will be welcomed and find a family like they've maybe never known.

Younger couples, years behind you, will find a living example of how hard and good marriage truly is.

The lost, the broken, the lonely, unbelievers—they'll be mesmerized as they see what an unbreakable kind of love looks like in a world where relationships are dropped as soon as it gets hard.

Your marriage will be like an incredible painting, on display for the world around you to see. And, when they look at it, they'll be able to say, "Wow, I didn't know God was this good."

Our Prayer for You

Father,

We pray that you would strengthen and deepen the marriages of our friends, the readers. We pray their marriage would be Jesus-focused, Spirit-led, and used to display the gospel of Jesus to everyone around. We pray that as each spouse serves, forgives, shows grace, and places courage in the other, You would be honored. Through hard times and sweet times, we pray this marriage would endure to the end.

Thank You for Your constant help, perfect wisdom, and immeasurable grace in each of our lives.

We pray all of this in faith, and in the name of Jesus.

Amen.

Acknowledgments

We both know that putting any creative project out into the world takes a complete team effort. This book you hold in your hands wouldn't be in existence without the incredible people who have believed in this project as much as us and even more than us at times.

Over the course of our marriage, we have been surrounded by some amazing couples who love God fiercely and seek to complement each other in their marriages. We wouldn't be who we are without seeing healthy marriages lived out in front of us. Most of them, a decade or two ahead of us, have given us the courage to fight for a beautiful marriage. We won't list their names, but they'll know who they are. Thank you.

We both work with people who push us to be our best selves. Lyndsey and Brice, thank you for helping to free us up so that we can do all that we've been created to do. Thanks to the incredible Austin Stone staff and

Creative Team for constantly pushing us forward in creativity and in seeking Jesus with our whole hearts. The elders of The Austin Stone continually cheered us on, and kept us aimed at the Word of God as we wrote this.

Jenni Burke, our delightful and fierce Literary Agent, this will always be the book that came to life at a beautiful villa in Italy. You are a dream to work with. To all of our team at B&H, thank you for believing in this project from the get-go. Lawrence, Taylor, Ashley, Mary, Jennifer, Jenaye, Devin—you guys are rock stars!

We are basically the luckiest people in the world because we have so many fabulous friends cheering us on. Halim Suh, Greg Brazaele, and Zach Varrett, thanks for the feedback, critique and writing help. Aaron wrote most of this book in Marfa, Texas, with his side-kick Alex Espinoza. Thanks for the helpful conversations about singleness and marriage that formed many sections of this book.

Annie and Kyle Lent, Kevin and Leslie Peck, Halim and Angela Suh, Ross and Sue Lester—your love and excitement for this project are over the top crazy and humbling! Thank you!

Cayden, Amos, Deacon and Story, our house wouldn't be as fun without you, and our prayer is that this book shows the world something you've seen us live out every day. We hope you'll believe that God loves marriage, and desires for us to complement each other as we give our lives away because of the gospel. May that be true of all of us.

Jesus, we're still in awe that you would love us so perfectly and unconditionally. We've learned everything we know about marriage from you. Your love for Your Bride, the Church, is the kind of love we're aiming for in our own marriage. Let us reflect You in all that we do.

About the Authors

 aron and Jamie Ivey live in Austin, Texas, where they parent four kids and do their best to change the world from right where they are. Jamie Ivey hosts the podcast, *The Happy Hour with Jamie Ivey*, has written some books, and will stop anything for some 90's hip hop. Aaron is a pastor at The Austin Stone, a songwriter, has written some books, and loves spending time cooking in the kitchen. Together they host the podcast, *On the Other Side*. They both believe that stories have such a huge impact on the world and are honored to share their story and lives with others.

ALSO FROM AARON & JAMIE IVEY

A 7-Session Bible Study

Does your marriage feel stuck in a rut? Do you feel like you and your spouse are never on the same team? Do you want a flourishing and vibrant marriage that reflects the gospel?

Over 7 sessions, the *Complement* Bible study shines a compelling light on the beauty of marriage as God intends it. Through biblical teaching, storytelling, and real-life examples, Aaron and Jamie Ivey dismantle the distorted cultural views of submission, servanthood, and leadership within a marriage and offer a better view of healthy, godly marriage. In this study, participants will walk through the purpose of marriage as the Scripture relates it and tackle topics such as family mission, sex, leadership, fighting, and forgiveness. Because marriage is meant to not only give life and hope to both husband and wife, but also point the world to Christ.

Available Wherever Books Are Sold.